ALWAYS CONNECT

How newsletters build influence, grow profits and make business fun again in today's digital world

by Simon Payn

Published in the United States and Canada by
Pin Mill Publishing
ISBN 978-0-9948662-0-2

For information visit **www.AlwaysConnectBook.com**

To BL

TABLE OF CONTENTS

Get Your Free Newsletter Toolkit

Go to **www.AlwaysConnectBook.com** and get your free newsletter toolkit – everything you need to make your own newsletter. You'll get

- Step-by-step guide to making your own newsletter with ready-made questionnaires and templates that will help you discover…
  - Your ideal client profile
  - What your customers are willing to pay premium fees for
  - What your customers would love to hear from you
  - How to connect personally with your customers
  - How to create a brand that customers love
  - Your easy newsletter publishing calendar
  - 10 easy article starters
  - The easy method for creating content … without writing
  - How to find and hire writers you'll love
- Ready-to-use print newsletter template
- Ready-to-use email newsletter template

Plus, discover how you can get Ready to Go Newsletters' ready-made newsletter service absolutely free for 30 days! Go to **www.AlwaysConnectBook.com**

INTRODUCTION

Remember those old-fashioned hardware stores? You know, the kind where the shelves are crammed floor to ceiling with tools, doorknobs, buckets and brooms, and the staff needs a rolling library ladder to reach the thing you want?

It's a bit dusty inside. But it's warm; it smells like fresh earth and sawdust. And best of all, you're a valued customer. The owner knows you by name—and your kids, and maybe even the dog.

The two of you chat while you wait for the clerk to cut your keys, or find the flower pot in the exact size you need. Small talk. "How's the family?" "Going to the game on Saturday?" And "Say, you should see this great new ladder I picked up at the hardware show—might be just what you need to clean out those gutters. And with spring coming, you'd better get to it!"

You know he's right—it's a real pain to deal with the gutters once the rain starts. Last month he was right about that ratchet set, and the month before he knew exactly what you meant when you asked for a "plumbing doohickey." And your friendly chat is likely to end with the sale of a ladder.

There's something charming about this. Old school. The hardware store owner knows you, you know him. He knows his stock and what to sell you—after all, he's an expert in hardware! He's served up helpful advice even when it turned out you didn't need to buy something after all. There's a relationship, a level of trust.

Take a moment and enjoy that feeling. Because that's the kind of relationship I want you to have with your clients...but in the modern world.

These days, your clients are more likely to click a button than hand you cash to ring up. You may not know their names. They may have found you from a recommendation or walking by your office, but more likely they've gotten a referral or read an online review. Maybe they found you by typing in "Service + City." How can you possibly build a relationship on pixels? How can you create trust, establish your expertise, and become the first choice, go-to provider when your client may not even know they need you?

NEWSLETTERS ROCK

Newsletters speak to your passion—which is your business. Newsletters engage your customers. They're proven. And they're cost-effective.

Done well, newsletters express genuineness in a world where everyone and no one is your "friend." The personal connection of a good newsletter creates real relationships in a world where everyone "likes" everything, and people "share" too much.

Newsletters can seem a little dusty in themselves. In a world of Facebook memes, retweets and Google-ad clicks, what place does a newsletter have nowadays? Are we really talking about trifolding an 8.5x11" sheet and stuffing envelopes?

As a recovering journalist who's learned marketing from the best, I can honestly say that newsletters can re-create the kind of customer connection that was so successful in the days of market squares and general stores—but with a very modern twist. Today, this timeless method of building connections between you and your customers is enhanced by using the Internet. From lead generation and building a database of recipients to driving traffic and measuring a newsletter's effectiveness, this way of creating loyal customers owes much of its ease-of-use to today's technology.

This book is about newsletters—and their 21st century electronic cousins. Why you need them, what to do with them and how to make them work for you.

FASTER HORSES
If I had asked people what they wanted,
they would have said faster horses.
- Henry Ford

When was the last time you visited a new restaurant? How did you choose it? You might have read an online review or heard a recommendation from a friend. Maybe you saw an article in the paper about a new bistro, and hey, you'd never have thought Malaysian food...I'd like to try Malaysian food...but the picture looked good and why not?

It's not always about finding out what your customers want. People often don't know what they want until you tell them—as Henry Ford says above, they'd have asked for faster horses rather than conceiving of the automobile. They don't know your product or service can make their life better until they hear about it. And with the rise of the Internet review, the TV guru and the radio expert, consumers are ever more reliant on 'experts' to tell them how and where to spend their money.

Everyone wants someone (anyone?) else to decide for them, for better or worse. Sometimes this means paying attention to word-of-mouth—other times it's clicking on that ad for One Easy Trick to Shrink Belly Fat. Remember Who Wants to be a Millionaire? Contestants who didn't know the answer could "phone a friend" or even "ask the audience." They were willing to bet all the cash they'd amassed up to that point, on someone else's best guess. They're desperate for someone to tell them how to answer the million-dollar question.

The show's producers called these "lifelines." And reaching out to someone else—whether it's an audience you hope will be mostly right, or your friend Jim who knows everything about the World Series—means getting some help. Feeling more secure about your choice. And the more we perceive someone as an 'expert' the readier we are to accept their recommendation on what we need.

Your newsletter establishes you as an expert. It's a vehicle to distribute your knowledge to people who are interested in hearing what you have to say. Over time, articles build on articles and advice on advice—proving to readers that you know your stuff and you can be trusted.

The Internet and the printed page add authority to your advice and opinions. The visual and mental impact of blog posts and videos makes you stand out: you become the go-to expert. By sharing knowledge and information your clients didn't know they needed, you show that you have your clients' best interests in mind. Instead of going for the quick, one-time sale, you build a relationship.

You build trust.

NEWSLETTERS WORK

Who says? Well, I think these stats show the effectiveness of "content marketing," which includes newsletters as well as several other channels. We'll discuss content marketing further in Chapter Six—I don't love the term "content," but sometimes it's the easiest way to describe what you're going to be sharing with your customers. For the moment, we'll focus on the proof of newsletters' impact. Imagine you've got ten people standing outside your business, debating whether or not to come in, and apply these percentages.

- According to research from www.marketingprofs.com, some 82% of consumers feel more positive about a company after reading useful information that's targeted directly to them. Eight of those ten people like your business better now.

- 90% of consumers find curated content useful. Nine of those potential customers think of you when they use your advice or information.

- Per dollar spent, content marketing generates approximately three times as many leads as traditional marketing. Each of those ten people has three friends you might be able to reach, too.

- Even better, it costs 62% less than traditional marketing. And you like saving money as much as your customers do.

WHAT YOU'LL LEARN

As we embark on this journey together, along the way you'll come across some really helpful information that will allow you to find your story, get it out there, and use that story to truly connect with your customers. Here's just a sample:

- What your "Why" is
- How to banish the "Elephant on the Balance Sheet" and the "Monsters in the Dark"
- Where to find the old-fashioned hardware store
- YMS+YGS = HLC (Your Magic Story plus Your Great Service equals Hugely Loyal Customers)
- How to become the go-to expert
- How auto-responders can actually enhance the personal connection
- The value of the compound customer

In the case studies you'll find throughout the book, you'll also notice that rather than diminishing newsletters, technology is enhancing them. These days you can almost reach out and touch your customer—but at their convenience. While you're building an old-fashioned relationship through newsletters, modern technology is making it so much easier to take your story and your business to the next level. We'll talk more about the actual resources and tools in Part Two.

HOW YOU'LL LEARN

There's an exercise at the end of every chapter, designed to help you adapt the advice in this book for your business and your personal story. Take some time with these. Scribble down some ideas. Think about it while you're waiting in the checkout line, or at the bank. If you take on and complete the challenge of these exercises, you'll know your story, how to share it, and how to turn that relationship into sales by the end of this book.

Throughout the book, I'll use case studies from successful businesses that show you these tools and techniques at work in the real world. You'll find some checklists to help you easily know what to do—and what not to do!

As I'll say at the end of every chapter, if you have questions, comments, suggestions, compliments or criticisms, just email me. Really! I hope you now know that this is my passion—the reason I get up in the morning. And I want to share it with you. Not so you'll become a client of my newsletter company—although you're certainly welcome—but because I want you to be able to build your own newsletter that reflects your personality and your passion.

I'm going to tell you how to do that. And somewhere along the way, I want you to have an "Aha!" moment about what newsletters can do for you.

My own "Aha" moment happened when I realized that my journalism education and experience, a strong antipathy for bosses, and a fascination with marketing were all pointing me to starting my own newsletter company. I did...and Ready to Go Newsletters products are read by about 250,000 people each month across the USA and Canada.

I love newsletters. My job here is to convince you that this is Absolutely the Best Way to "Make" Loyal Customers. You're going to discover:

- how to build a relationship with your current customers, such that they'll never look any farther than you

- how to attract new customers who are looking for your specific service
- how to create customers who didn't even know they needed your service
- and how to do all of this genuinely and with passion

It's a tall order. But I firmly believe in newsletters, and I'm betting you'll be a believer, too. By the end of this book—if not before—you'll understand what a newsletter has to offer your business, know what to include in your own newsletter, and be ready to take the first steps to grow your loyal customer base.

JUST THE FACTS

Maybe you want to be trusted and you want to build relationships and grow your customer base, but you have some questions:

Won't writing and distributing a newsletter be a lot of time and effort?

Not as much as you think. Once you get started, a regular calendar and a set format will make your newsletter easy to fill in each time. There are also services (like mine) that can do them for you. We'll talk more about the actual mechanics in Part Two.

Is this really going to help my business?

Yes. I'll quote you some more statistics in Chapter Two, but let's do the fun part first.

How am I going to learn to do this?

By reading this book, and trying the real-world exercises at the end of each chapter. When you have the right newsletter, it's an extension and support of what you already do. We'll talk more about how your newsletter reflects your business in Chapter Seven. And feel free to email me with comments and questions!

Visit **www.AlwaysConnectBook.com** to claim your free newsletter toolkit—everything you need to make your own newsletter… easily and stress-free.

PART 1

What Is Your Why?

Chapter 1

You went into business on your own for a reason, right? You know that you want to spend your day doing something you care about instead of whiling away your life in a cubicle. It takes a special kind of person to become—and stay—an entrepreneur. Like me, you're working from sale to sale and contract to contract. Walking away from your business just means shutting the door or turning down that next opportunity. Every day you wake up with the option to quit.

But you don't.

Most entrepreneurs are not in it solely for the money. Sure, we all want to eat, provide for our families, live in nice surroundings and pay off the car. But we could get those things from jobs that wouldn't demand even half as much time, focus, energy…and heart.

Entrepreneurs have passion for their work. You care about it—more than you might care about someone else's business where you're merely an employee—and you enjoy sharing that passion with the world. That connection fuels your soul.

A newsletter gives you a vehicle to share your passion, to connect directly with the people you serve, and provides you with the opportunity to make your clients' and prospects' lives better. Plus, you're building relationships. You give (and that feels good) but you also get. (And that feels even better.)

Finally, it makes your work—your life!—that much more fulfilling. And if you do it right, it makes other people's lives more fulfilling as well. But what does "doing it right" mean?

People don't buy what you do; they buy why you do it. And what you do simply proves what you believe.

- Simon Sinek, *Start with Why: How Great Leaders Inspire Everyone to Take Action*

"Doing it right" is all about finding your story and sharing it with your customers. People don't buy what you do, they buy why you do it. And defining—and sharing—your Why helps you find, create, and connect with customers.

This isn't my idea. It belongs to Simon Sinek—a true visionary, in my opinion. Here's how it works: Lots of people sell insurance. Lots of people sell real estate. Lots of people sell whatever it is you have to sell. And lots of people need what you have to offer. Should be an easy match, but we all know it's just not that simple.

To stand out from the crowd and become the go-to expert in your town, you need to do more than match your commodity to people who are looking for it. Sinek goes on to say that the goal is not to do business with people who need what you have—the goal is to do business with people who believe what you believe. But how can you find those people, and figure out whether their beliefs and yours are a good match?

You probably have lots of logical ideas about why people should buy real estate, insurance or whatever you make, and why they should buy it from you. But your customers and potential customers really don't want to hear those technical reasons. Our brains are wired to respond to emotions, not logic. If you can express the mission—the emotional Whys—behind what you do, your passionate Whys will slice straight through to the limbic brain, bypassing the rational mind. And that's a good thing, because it destroys the competition; they're still targeting their pitch to the logical mind.

Take a moment and go check out Simon Sinek's TED talk, "Start With Your Why." It's about 18 minutes long, and worth every second. Go to: www.tinyurl.com/S-Sinek

THE GOLDEN CIRCLE

Most people communicate from the outside in. We describe what we can provide and how we can provide it, and we leave that messy why to the very end, where we can sort of gloss over it. Leaders, on the other hand, start with the Why. They start with what they believe.

In Simon Sinek's TED talk (you checked that video out, right? Go do it now, I'll be here when you get back) he discusses how great leaders communicate in exactly the opposite way from the rest of us. They start with the Why. Simon Sinek uses the Golden Circle to represent the process of looking inward from the What, through the How, to get to the Why.

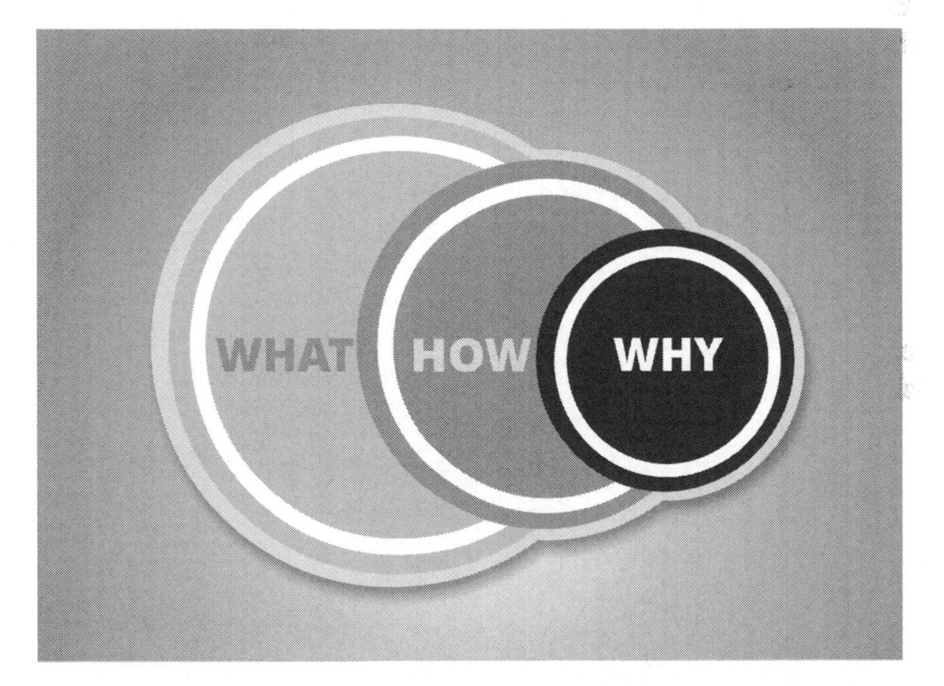

What product or service do you deliver? How do you get it to your customers? And why do they need it? The first two questions are easy to answer—your What is sitting in boxes in your stockroom or showing up as a line item on an invoice; your How is your physical store, your office, or the website where clients find you. But knowing Why takes a little more thought. It's not a physical process—it's an emotional conviction.

Finding your Why is finding the underlying motivation for being in the business you're in. What drives your passion for the work. When you're motivated, the less-exciting stuff you have to do to make your business function (like bookkeeping or cold calls) can start to have real meaning. That meaning transfers through your marketing to your clients.

CASE STUDY: APPLE COMPUTER

Apple has built a brand on the premise that everything the company does must challenge the status quo. They've stayed true to that belief—as one Wells Fargo analyst put it recently, "Apple has historically never done anything because someone told them to do something—they do what they think is right, and they go down that path." Challenging the status quo is Apple's Why.

In practice, Apple challenges the status quo by manufacturing computers that are beautifully designed and easy to use. Maybe all your music should fit in your pocket. Maybe your phone should show movies. Apple creates those technologies and packs them into a compact and attractive form—that's their How.

Finally, Apple addresses the What, almost as though it's an after-thought: Would you like to buy one?

By the time a consumer arrives in Apple's store, they're often already sold—they're in the store to pick memory-size options and choose colors, not to make up their mind about whether they want the product. Every model of the iPhone has had crowds lining up to buy it, willing to wait outside in the cold to give Apple their money.

If we believe in the need for a better-designed computer that's also user-friendly and pleasing to look at (at first a huge change from the status quo), we'll buy an Apple. Not because the company wants us to, but because we buy into the need to change the status quo, as expressed by the company. Apple shares the message, we're rebels, and even now that their computers and phones are in wide release, owning a Mac instead of a PC is not just a tech choice, it's a statement. Desk-bound corporate drones type on PCs. Scrappy, creative start-up types hog the outlets at the coffee shop with their shiny silver MacBook Airs. Sure, it's a stereotype—but it's also a powerful expression of Apple's Why. It's not just a computer—it's a badge of creativity.

This feeling of connection to a company's Why leads to not only great sales, but great relationships. Most businesses end up focusing on the What, because it's the immediate thing they deal with every day—I have widgets, I need to sell widgets, wouldn't you like to buy a widget? The What feels faster. It feels like the job that has to be done before you can even sit down and think about why. But sharing your mission—your Why—with your customers helps you lead them. Not just to your services, but to a better life. To expressing their Why with your product or service.

FINDING YOUR WHY

Deep down, hidden under the suit and behind the professional facade, there are real reasons why we get into the businesses we do. There is a reason why we get up in the morning apart from having to pay the bills. And it's not always about pursuing riches and prestige. Fame and fortune is a result that comes from what we do, not the underlying reason why we do it.

> Knowing your why is the first step in figuring out how to achieve the goals that excite you and create a life you enjoy living (versus merely surviving!) ...Only when you know your 'why' will you find the courage to take the risks needed to get ahead,

> stay motivated when the chips are down, and move your life onto a new, more challenging, and more rewarding trajectory.
>
> - Margie Warrell, contributor to Forbes Online

As entrepreneurs, we're driven to do what we believe. So what is your real reason? What do you believe? Usually, this belief is not out in plain sight, driving you to succeed no matter what. That's because we're all so busy getting on with the day-to-day stuff that we kind of forget we have passion.

How do you find your passion, your mission, your Why? There's an exercise at the end of this chapter to help you get to your specific, personal Why, but you can start that process now by focusing on the value you add.

Where in the transaction process do you add value? What is it that you provide that makes peoples' lives better? Some examples:

- If you're in real estate, you're helping people find environments that will allow them and their families to thrive.

- If you're in insurance, you're protecting people from disaster and making them happier because they have the peace of mind that insurance coverage provides.

- In the mortgage business, you're making it possible for people to achieve their dreams and put a roof over their heads.

- Financial planners are taking the fear out of retirement. They're ensuring that people have adequate savings and investments, so they won't have to spend their retirement years in poverty.

- And you accountants? Well, you're helping people live more fruitful lives, saving them money that they can spend on things that really mean something.

CASE STUDY: SIMON PAYN'S WHYS

Here's a personal example: my Whys. These are the reasons I get up in the morning, and why writing, selling, and maximizing the impact of newsletters is the right job for me—the What that springs directly from my Whys.

I want to help my clients to become 'famous' in their markets, so that when people think of real estate, insurance, accounting, fruit baskets, or whatever it is my client provides, they'll think of my client first.

I want to help my clients build life-long, satisfying relationships with people who know them, like them and trust them.

I want my clients to experience people coming to them for business, rather than having to go out and hunt down business.

I want my clients to enjoy marketing their businesses by sharing their knowledge and experience with others.

I want my clients to feel secure, knowing that they have a list of people who want to do business with them.

I want my clients to love their work, because they will be in a business built on long-term satisfying relationships. I want them to be as passionate about their Why as I am.

YOUR MISSION

A mission is a statement of purpose—the reason my company, and yours, exists. Generally speaking, it's a guideline for decision-making of all kinds. It forms a roadmap for the company to follow in all the activities it undertakes, and a guide in strategic decision-making. When you know your company's purpose, it's much easier to strategize. You can always look at a hard choice and ask, "How will this help us achieve our mission?"

From thinking about value added, and what I want my clients to experience, I've developed a mission statement that formalizes my Whys. My mission is simple, but challenging (as a mission must be). It is to help businesses succeed, grow and prosper, while fulfilling the goals and dreams of the entrepreneurs who started them.

Ready To Go Newsletters' Mission

To develop newsletters that people want to read.

To banish painful cold-calling by encouraging your clients to reach out to you first.

To allow you to share your expertise with the world

To help you build a business with a solid foundation of clients who like and respect you.

To help you get more joy from your business by living with an attitude of service.

To help businesses succeed, grow and prosper, while fulfilling the goals and dreams of the entrepreneurs who started them.

Without a doubt, from the day I figured this out I've felt good about my business. I wasn't just making newsletters; I was making a valuable contribution. And here's where it gets strange: when I started to think like that, my business started to grow rapidly.

My enthusiasm and my desire to help must have rubbed off on the people I emailed and spoke with. I wasn't just trying to sell...I was trying to help. My customers could feel that, and it made them want to do business with me, the guy who wanted to help them. And so I made more money. Ironic, isn't it? The more we focus on genuinely serving our customers, the more we see an impact on the bottom line.

I know that newsletters are powerful. But I also know that, for various reasons, most people don't send them. So I decided I was there to make using newsletters easy. To provide a service that helped other business grow and prosper. This is what helps me get up and get to work in the morning: the thought that I am helping other business owners achieve their goals.

OVERCOMING THE FEAR OF WHY

Being able to articulate your mission is great. But knowing it yourself is only half the story; the other half is sharing your Why with your clients. Which, of course, is easier said than done. For a start, you've got to meet the challenge of fear. Do any of these sound familiar?

- I don't think anyone really cares why I'm in this business.
- People might think my "mission" is silly or pretentious.
- I don't want to share my personal philosophy with strangers.
- I don't have time to find my Why, I'm too busy selling my What.

At the root of each of these mental objections is fear. Fear of apathy, fear of mockery, fear of putting ourselves out there, fear of spending time on something that doesn't feel like selling-widgets-right-now.

These fears are stopping us from doing anything different or innovative. We constantly hark back to the same boring, sterile, faceless marketing that our competition is doing. It's a frightening prospect to actually get a bit personal with our clients and prospects. Making our business something we truly believe in increases our perception of risk. Now we're not just putting out a widget—we're putting out ourselves. It's easy to be afraid of what people will think.

Don't be. If you have a service that makes the lives of your clients better, that helps them save money or time, that makes them more efficient and happier, then it's your duty to market that service and sell your clients on the benefits of that service.

And as for finding the time, I can assure you that time spent finding your Why is one of the most valuable investments you can make in your own business.

CASE STUDY: SHARPEN YOUR SAW

Yes, it's parable time.

A Buddhist monk walking through the forest comes upon a man trying to saw down a tree. But the lumberjack's saw is dull, and it's taking a long time.

The monk gently suggests, "Why don't you stop and sharpen your saw?"

The lumberjack retorts, "I have to cut down this tree! I don't have time to stop and sharpen my saw!"

Thinking about your Why is sharpening your saw. When you've got a clear handle on why you want to be doing the business you're doing, you'll feel more motivated about attacking your day-to-day pile of Whats.

You'll know which tasks and goals are the most important, and which can be left behind. You'll be ready to get up in the morning and carry out your Why.

BOREDOM IS YOUR FRIEND

Most people are bored. As Henry David Thoreau said, "Most men lead lives of quiet desperation and go to the grave with the song still in them." Now that's a downer. And an opportunity.

Think about what you can you do to make your marketing—and therefore the lives of the people who come into contact with it—less gray and more interesting. What can you do to make them think or to make them smile? How can your newsletter create a time to relax and feel supported by your expertise? Or a moment of fun? And how can that connection become an opportunity for your service to enhance their life?

CASE STUDY: HIS DAUGHTER'S JOKE

Here's a real estate agent who sensed the opportunity to make his clients' lives happier. He won my Newsletter Marketer of the Year contest a couple of years ago, and I'm happy to say he's still a client. He writes:

"With newsletters I know I am tending to my farm area, which is 700 households. Every month I walk the newsletters to most of them. I distribute another 100 or so by mail and hand them out at open houses and to for-sale-by-owners. I have also connected to local business owners by including gift certificates and coupons in the newsletter. For fun, I include a joke from my young daughter most months.

Something silly, like:

What did the zero say to the eight?

"Nice belt," or

What did one math book say to another?

"I have a lot of problems."

The kind of joke a mom could tell her kid when she picks him up after school.

I also constantly talk about supporting local businesses and growing your own food and eating out of your garden. This theme is ever expanding. I even take fresh-grown herbs to houses.

The biggest benefit is meeting people as I walk the neighborhood distributing the newsletters. One month I left out my daughter's joke and a man stopped me to offer his friendly "complaint"—he missed the joke! We had a great conversation, and

I'm looking forward to helping him sell his house.

Through the newsletter I am able to become a "brand," because I concentrate on what I am about other than real estate.

This client figured out his Why, and even more importantly, he's living it. His clients have no difficulty figuring out what he's about.

Or working with him.

THE REAL YOU

In a world where it's impossible to tell what is real and what is not, you have a chance to stand out by proving your authenticity. Unlike faceless corporations, you are you. And, as you'll find out in the upcoming chapters, by using a newsletter, you can prove it.

That's why we encourage our clients to tweak their newsletters a little to include something personal and local. Something that shows a little bit of you, and your Why.

Like the successful real estate agent above who includes his young daughter's jokes in his newsletter, supports local businesses and takes fresh herbs to his newsletter recipients, you too can brand yourself using your Why and your Unique Selling Proposition, which we'll discuss at length in Chapter 3.

THE TAKEAWAY

Finding your Why helps you commit to your business and your customers commit to you. It gives purpose to getting up in the morning and going to work.

Given your Why, you can learn to love all those tasks that are part and parcel of running your business. Even—or maybe especially—your newsletter. Instead of seeing it as a chore, consider it as a way to spread your expertise to many people. A labor of love. A way of bringing pleasure by making something people want to read (if you do it right). And instead of viewing it as a waste of time, realize that you will get praise from clients who like your newsletter, many of whom may decide to do business with you because of it.

EXERCISE: FINDING YOUR WHY

Here's how to find your Why—and use it to attract many more clients or customers than you had before.

Finding your Why isn't a quick process, and your Why may evolve. So think long and hard about it, write down your conclusions and revisit them frequently. Spend the time you need. This exercise may change the course of your business—and your life—so isn't it worth it?

1) Decide what you stand for. What are you passionate about?

Think about what you care about. What do you want the world to have more of (more food grown locally, stronger support for local business, happy and secure families in houses they love)? Or what do you want the world to have less of (gray, boring, faceless marketing, hard-to-use computers, trouble finding a local serviceperson)?

2) Think about how your business fits in with your thoughts in Question 1.

How does what you do or provide help give the world more, or solve a problem? How does your passion fuel what you do at work each day?

3) Statistics show that people prefer to work with people they know, like and trust. So how can you find ways of showing that you're likeable and trustworthy?

Decide what you want to reveal about yourself. Do you like sharing personal stories, or news tidbits, or making sure everyone in town knows about an event? Do you have specialized knowledge about a problem many people deal with, but few know how to solve? Are you always up-to-date on the latest scoop in your industry? You don't have to share your whole life, but think of a couple of personal or unique elements that will help your customers connect with your business. What can you express with genuine, personal enthusiasm?

4) Fill in the blanks:

My mission in this life is to

____

____

My business serves this mission by

____

____

I know I have succeeded in my mission when my customers experience

____

____

Hang onto these answers as you move through the rest of the book. They—or some version of them—are your Why. How you show that Why becomes your brand.

For example, a yoga teacher might realize that her mission is to help people experience greater physical health and emotional calm in life. Her business serves this mission by providing classes at both introductory and more advanced levels to reach as many people as possible; employing teachers with a genuine commitment to the mission; and having a calm, pleasant environment in the studio. She knows she's succeeded when her clients mention a greater sense of well-being, commit to regular attendance, and when she sees them accomplish poses that were challenging for them in previous classes. Her brand will reflect a sense of calm accomplishment. And those two words, calm and accomplishment, give her a wealth of subject matter to explore in a newsletter. Wouldn't you read something short every other week about being calm and having a sense of accomplishment?

Once you've established your personal Why and how you'll use it to effectively brand yourself, you're ready to move on to the next two chapters.

In Chapter Two, we'll see how you can create loyal fans, and use your Why to acquire more customers who identify with your brand and help you fulfill your Why—while buying your product or hiring your service.

Let me know if you have questions, comments, suggestions, compliments or criticisms. You can email me by visiting this book's website at **www.AlwaysConnectBook.com**. I will get back to you.

Because helping you succeed is my Why.

The Theory Of Compound Customers

CHAPTER 2

And there it is: planet Earth at its height. Covered with megacities, five moons, population 96 billion. The hub of a galactic domain, stretching across a million planets, a million species.

With mankind right in the middle...

- The Doctor, from Doctor Who

Wow. That's a lot of potential customers.

- Simon Payn

OK, I know—not all these billions are future customers. But some will be. Whether you're selling a product or a service, there are people who buy from you now and people who might buy from you in the future. These individuals are the reason your business grows—or doesn't grow.

Which brings me to my Theory of Compound Customers: The importance of returning clients, who in turn bring you more customers through positive word of mouth, and active referrals. Even dragging their friends in to buy your product because your customers know it will make their friends lives' better—just like it did for them! I'm calling this concept The Theory of Compound Customers, and once you embrace it, you'll never fail to keep in touch with your clients again.

If you think about the compound interest that accrues in your savings account—where interest builds up on interest—you'll recall why you stuck your money in that savings account to begin with. Because in the long term—even with today's low rates—your money will grow faster in your savings account than if you stashed your cash under the mattress, thanks to compound interest. It's a no-brainer, right?

It works exactly the same way with clients.

If you encourage clients to come back again and again, while continuing to attract new clients, your overall income goes up…almost exponentially.

YRC+YNC=BMEG

Your Repeat Customers + Your New Customers =
Big, Maybe Exponential, Growth

WHY FLORISTS NEED NEWSLETTERS

You might not be a florist, but take a moment and imagine yourself surrounded by roses. Isn't that soothing? Relax for a moment, and let's talk compounding. Enjoy this quiet moment, because once you embrace the Theory of Compound Customers, you'll never fail to keep in touch with your clients again.

If you're a florist, Your Repeat Customers walk in, buy some flowers, get them wrapped or vased or however they want to present them to their loved one, and you see them again on the next major holiday. Why would florists need newsletters?

Making YRCs

Say you're a florist. It's 5 pm on February 14, and this guy walks in. He needs flowers for his wife, and he just happens to pick you because your store is on his way home. No bonus points, no loyalty card, he just saw the roses in the window, realized what day it was and cut across four lanes of traffic to walk in your door. He picks out a dozen roses, you break out the baby's breath and ferns and help him pick a card, he's relieved you saved his marriage, and that's $40 in the cash register, thank you very much. Off goes the customer.

Now, will this customer need flowers again? Probably. Next February 14, at the very least. But will he come back to you? Maybe. Or maybe not, given the competition from online florists. Maybe he'll remember fast enough to hit the flower shop next to the office instead of you on the way home.

Worst-Case Scenario: $40 earned, one visit.

What would happen if you encouraged this client to come back by sending him a newsletter to remind him in advance of Valentine's Day, and hey, Mother's Day, Christmas, a table arrangement for Thanksgiving, and some don't-forget dates like birthdays and anniversaries?

Do you think he'd come back to you more often? He might even buy more flowers instead of other gifts for special days. Imagine you get him back next year for Valentine's Day and Mother's Day.

Customer becomes Your Repeat Customer: $120 earned, three visits.

Then imagine he comes every year for the next five years. (After all, why would he go anywhere else? Your flowers are good, and now he gets reminders of when to buy them.)

Your Repeat Customer enjoys happy relationships: $400 in your pocket, 10 visits.

Better-Case Scenario: You've gone from a $40 sale to a $520 sale, just by keeping in touch.

Now, imagine that this happens to each of the new clients who walked in that fateful Valentine's Day. Say it was a busy day, and you sold a bouquet of flowers to each of the 50 new people who came in. You would have earned $2,000. Not bad.

Best-Case Scenario: If they kept coming back (like the first buyer), you would have earned $26,000. That's an extra $24,000—13 times as much.

We're using floristry as an example, but the concept relates to every business and professional service. Every day you fail to keep in touch with clients is money left on the table.

THE ELEPHANT ON THE BALANCE SHEET

One of the truest—and saddest—facts of business is this: most profits are made from existing customers, not new ones.

The sad part is that many businesses fail to get that second sale. Let's put on our customer hat. How often do you buy something, have a very happy experience, and then never hear from that business again? Can we say 95% of the time? And when it happens, don't you feel hollow? Just a little pang of But I really liked you! Didn't you really like me?

To me, not following through with a customer borders on rudeness—like you don't care after you've taken their money. No matter how big the business, not following up means failing to sell to existing clients—and that means leaving thousands of dollars on the table.

More to the point: It's a giant waste. Research from Constant Contact indicates that it costs a minimum of six times more hard-earned cash to attract a new customer than to service an existing one. And that isn't even acknowledging the fact that repeat customers spend at least 60% more than new customers.

Consider this: You've already spent hundreds of dollars and hours of your time to attract clients in the first place. You have to find them and they have to find you; then you have to establish your trustworthiness; and finally you have to provide a great customer experience to get that first sale.

So it only makes sense that once you've got them in your sphere of influence, you can sell to them again and again without that massive up-front acquisition cost.

Newsletters help because they make it easy to keep in touch with past clients. Just collect their contact data and mail or email them with information that will make their lives better. If you make offers that match their interests, they'll be back to buy from you again. You can turn them from a single-visit customer into one of Your Repeat Customers.

YRC = YOUR REPEAT CUSTOMERS

Writing for Inc.com, marketing expert Victor Ho says, "For many small businesses, loyalty marketing may be the only marketing they need, because it builds upon their greatest asset: their most satisfied customers."

It's not exactly breaking news that you should look after your good customers to ensure they don't leave you for a competitor. Just about every management expert has something—usually a lot—to say about customer loyalty and how to gain it. Loyalty marketing programs abound (how many grocery store savings tags are on your keychain?). But I'm talking here about something different.

Customer loyalty isn't about tags or stamps or punchcards or points. Customer loyalty isn't a program or a scheme or Crazy Bonus Thursdays. Customer loyalty is when people choose to use your shop or buy your product as a deliberate choice instead of another option. I like this definition because it doesn't focus on programs or incentives to customers. After all, there's only so much room in our wallets for more frequent-shopper cards, and eventually they all blend together.

When customers are loyal, they choose you because they prefer to buy from you. It could be your location, or that it's where their mom used to shop, but you can't really control those things. What you can control is the number one reason customers choose one store over another:

Customer Service. The basic, old-fashioned value of putting the customer first.

Instead of a marketing strategy, let's focus on customer service. It's a lot less expensive than setting up a points plan, and just about anyone can offer it.

YNC = YOUR NEW CUSTOMERS

Now that you're convinced (hopefully) of the value of nurturing your loyal repeat customers, let's turn to the other side of the equation—Your New Customers.

While I agree with Victor Ho that marketing to repeat customers is especially vital to small businesses, I don't believe that's the only kind of marketing you'll need. There's great value in attracting new customers to the fold. In fact, I don't believe you can grow your business without them.

We've just seen how careful attention to Your Repeat Customers can give you incremental growth; statistically, about 20% per year. But don't put all your eggs in one basket!

What about faster growth? Massive growth, mega growth, breakthrough growth? What if you want to take over your entire market—fast!

To get revenue increases of 50%, 100%, or more... you're going to need more people buying your products and services—and lots of them.

- Paul Lemberg, Business Coach

Paul Lemberg also quotes a statistical model built by the respected product developer, Doug Hall. The model shows that new customers are 2.8 times more important to rapid revenue growth than repeat purchasers. Think about it: are you more likely to have each of your current customers double their spending, or be able to double your customer base? Probably the latter—and you can keep doing that every year. Which is pretty compelling evidence of the key role new customers play, isn't it?

The ideal (of course) is to focus on stable growth and maintaining the loyalty of existing customers, while still going after the big revenue hits of multiplying your customer base. The way to do this is to market to both new and repeat customers simultaneously.

YOU CAN HAVE IT ALL

The fly in the ointment for many small businesses has always been the fact that it costs more to market to new customers. Up to 16 times more, if Doug Hall's statistics are to be believed. How can a small business compete with the deep pockets of regional, national or even global corporations?

Well, I'm here to tell you that you can have it all. The solution for the small businessperson with a small advertising budget is simple: Build connections and important relationships with both old and new customers through a useful, interesting, customer-focused newsletter.

Let's look back at our florist friend. If he converts 50 new customers who bought bouquets from his store that Valentine's Day into repeat customers, by sending interesting, useful newsletters with reminders of upcoming flower-giving opportunities, his business will grow incrementally.

If he knows this: That very day, he'll get names and emails from the new customers so he can send them reminders and newsletters. If he'd had a chance to talk—it was a very busy day—he'd ask about their interests and perhaps jot those down beside their names and e-mails. He'd conscientiously do everything he could to establish that personal connection during and after the very first sale. And when better to do this?

Or, perhaps I should ask, when else? This is sort of a "duh" question. But it's surprising how many ambitious entrepreneurs fail to get it. Here you have a brand new customer who has just had a positive experience at your place of business. He or she is happy and has warm, fuzzy feelings about you. So what do you do? Wave goodbye and turn to the next customer?

If you just wave goodbye, the likelihood of that customer beating a path to your door again is slim to nil. It's not that they dislike you; it's because they're forgetful. Even though the experience was a positive one, they'll almost certainly forget about you because they're bombarded with choices. It's hard to keep them all in your head. It's hard to remember who's who and what's where. They're overwhelmed, and you've done nothing to remind them of their positive experience with your business.

FORGET-ME-NOT FOLLOWERS

Where did you go the last time you bought special occasion flowers? Can you remember without looking up your credit card statement? Had you ever been there before, or did you pick the florist 'on the way' to somewhere else? Or did you screech to a stop when you saw the FLOWERS sign, remembering that it was someone's birthday, or heaven forbid, your anniversary?

Think of your last Google search. Didn't you find that all those websites you visited turn into a kind of online soup in your head? Did you go back to the most useful one, or just the one with 'good enough' options you could remember when you got tired of looking? Or maybe even the one that emailed you the next day with "Hey, yesterday you browsed our site, and today we have a sale on the item you looked at."

It's no surprise that people forget to come back, even to a business that gave them a positive experience. They're not ignoring you. They're simply overwhelmed. And they're likely to choose the most convenient option at that moment instead of planning their purchase...unless they have a relationship.

So how do you build a relationship that is strong enough to put your customers among the 21% of people who decide they will stay with your company because they can't find what you offer anywhere else?

By offering the intangibles—the old-fashioned values. That's what your customers are looking for; the values that are absent in our high-tech low-touch marketplace. Even generations that do a ton of business on the internet via their phones—well, they're looking at review websites to pick a restaurant, or reading customer feedback on a product they're considering purchasing.

The hardware store owner (back in the Introduction, remember him?) offered intangibles. He responded to his customer's wants and needs—even when the customer himself didn't know he needed it: ("Say, you should see this great new ladder I picked up at the hardware show—might be just what you need to clean out the eavestroughing. And with spring coming, you'd better get to it.")

The hardware store owner pinpointed his customer's potential problem, supplied an answer and made a sale. He closed the sale not because he was pushy or trying to upsell the guy, but because he was genuinely delighted that he had a product to solve his customer's problem. He was proud he could help. To him, it was simply a chat between friends that ended up in a sale—and a happy customer. Win-win.

Try having that kind of a relationship with a computer, however sophisticated.

A newsletter helps by starting and then maintaining a relationship. If you can collect a prospect's information when they visit your website (or store), then you can contact them with a valuable newsletter to remind them that you're there, looking out for them. Whether they make an initial purchase or not, you can keep in touch so that they won't forget you the next time they need what you offer.

In a sea of choices, your newsletter is like a life raft. It's no wonder clients reach out to you.

THE TAKEAWAY

Repeat customers are easier and cheaper to market to, and it's important to build their loyalty. New customers are tougher and more expensive to get, but we need them for dramatic revenue increases. The way to reach both groups is by harking back to the days of old-fashioned, genuine customer service, building deep and trusting relationships by sharing and proving your expertise.

You don't need deep pockets to do this. Try a cost-effective, easy, and proven successful approach that works for both groups—newsletters.

THE EXERCISE

Here's another of my little charts. This one refers to real estate agents in particular, but the general idea applies to any business. While this doesn't include splitting commissions or payments to brokers, the conclusion is irrefutable: You earn a lot more money by keeping a client for your career.

To see how The Theory of Compound Customers works for you, follow these steps:

Put your numbers in place of the real estate agent's numbers. More than likely you have them at your fingertips. Think about how long you have been/will be in business, as well as the market for your product or service, and what your profit margin is, and put those in, too.

The chart above shows the difference in commission earned by a real estate agent who keeps clients for life compared to one who just does a single transaction with a client. The difference results in four times as much earned in commissions.

Here's how:

Consider that a real estate career lasts 30 years. And the average time a family spends in one house is up to seven years. So, over that 30 years, the family will move an average of four times (4 x 7 = 28).

If the median home price in the U.S. is $265,800[1], and the listing agent's commission is 3%, the commission earned would be $7,974. 4 sales = $31,896, a difference of $23,922.

So… How do your numbers stack up?

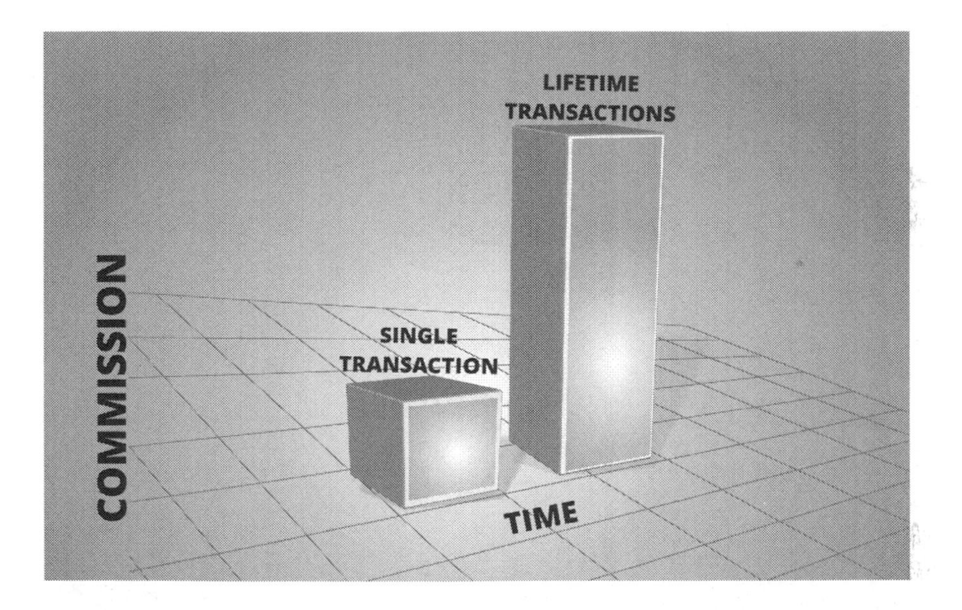

In Chapter 3, we'll look at how to share and prove your expertise through interesting, useful newsletters with a big dash of personality.

Don't forget. If you have comments or critiques or compliments send them along. You are my Whos and I genuinely care what you think. Find me at **www.AlwaysConnectBook.com**

1 http://www.globalpropertyguide.com/North-America/United-States/Price-History which quotes the U.S. census bureau.

"Trust Me..."

CHAPTER 3

"Trust me..."

No doubt about it, these two little words are the most over-valued in the Western world. These days, everyone talks about trust—from used-car salesmen and payday loan companies to politicians, to well, you and me. After all, who can we really trust? It has become almost a touchstone that the people you can trust least are the ones who tell you "trust me."

No wonder customers have trust issues!

Trust is at a premium these days. According to an Infosys whitepaper, a huge majority of consumers are still more comfortable sharing information face-to face, including some 70% of retail customers. You don't win your customers' trust by telling them how great your company is, or buying a bigger ad. You win it through personal connection; through proving your product, your advice, and yourself are there to make their lives better. We trust people when we feel like we know them—and their actions have proved they are looking out for us.

And without that trusting relationship? Well, here's a very scary statistic: Out of the customers who describe themselves as "satisfied" with their purchase, only 21% of them actually intend to maintain the buyer/seller relationship. So where are all the others going?

Marketing statistics suggest that many customers are doing their shopping elsewhere mainly because they say they simply don't trust the company they were doing business with previously. Why this lack of trust? As you know, customers these days are very demanding.

They're more price-sensitive than they ever were before and they're deal-shoppers; but at the same time, they want that unparalleled Customer Experience (as corporate marketers have dubbed it).

When they don't find it, they go. Some 82% of customers blamed a poor customer experience for leaving a company they had been doing business with, and (this hurts) 89% began doing business with a competitor after a poor customer experience. Their departure could have been triggered by not getting through to a human being on the phone, or not understanding how to use the product, or feeling like no one helped them in the store. In the final analysis, the customer not returning almost always had to do with the company's behaviour, and…wait for it…"poor communication."

It's a bummer, isn't it? This really isn't good news for ambitious entrepreneurs like us. We know we're reliable, honest, offer good value and great products, care about customers, etc., etc., etc. But how do we beat those odds? How do we prove our value to clients, both long-term and new? You provide a product that is similar to your competitors' products. So why should customers buy from you and not your competitors? There's really not much to differentiate you from them, is there?

Hopefully, yes there is. Your Repeat Customers can believe that they have and will continue to have a superior customer experience if they buy their commodity from you rather than the store across the street. Not the place with the deepest discounts, or the biggest signs—the place they trust.

Like the hardware store owner in the introductory chapter to this book, you need to build strong relationships based on trust with your customers. This is important in attracting new customers and essential in retaining current customers. And it's a key part of our equation, YRC + YNC = BMEG. So key that I'm going to repeat it:

YRC+YNC=BMEG
Your Repeat Customers + Your New Customers =
Big, Maybe Exponential, Growth

When you fail to follow up after an initial purchase or contact, you're not capitalizing on the opportunity to build a trusting relationship with that customer. It's one of the most widely accepted marketing facts: People do business with people they like and trust.

BUILDING CUSTOMER TRUST

Trust needs to be earned, by fulfilling promises and building relationships over the long term. Relationships build trust, and trust builds customer loyalty. To return to the question of why they should buy from you and not a competitor: This is why: you offer what your competitors don't.

A newsletter works as a tool to build those relationships of trust. It gives you a track record of providing valuable client-centered information and opens up opportunities for two-way communication. I believe your good customers (that 21%) trust that they have and will continue to have a superior customer experience if they buy their commodity from you rather than the website across the street.

So how do you build the kind of relationship strong enough to put your customers in that magic 21%? You offer the intangibles—the old-fashioned values. That's what your customers are looking for. As I've mentioned before, customers miss the values that are absent in our high-tech, low-touch marketplace.

Here are three essential rules for providing old-fashioned customer service, and those "tangible intangibles" customers are looking for:

RULE #1: ALWAYS PUT THE CUSTOMER FIRST

Ask yourself: What does he or she care about? How can I provide it?

Probably the most common mistake novice company newsletter publishers make is this: they write about the wrong person.

What do I mean by that? Simply, that it's not enough—and it's not effective—to write (or talk) about you, your company and your product or service. The fact is, while you are no doubt incredibly interesting to yourself, unfortunately, no one else shares your sentiments. OK, maybe your mom. But she's probably already your customer.

So while you'll want to include information about who you are and what you do in some way (that's what adds the personality), the bulk of the newsletter or any other marketing communications should be focused on things that will interest the reader. This doesn't mean you have to steer away completely from writing about your product or service. But instead of writing about the features of what you offer, **write about how your product or service will benefit the reader.**

- × Feature: Bob Smith has sold over 100 houses in Localtown!

- ✓ Benefit: With Bob Smith's experience selling over 100 Localtown houses, he'll be able to help you maximize the value of your home and sell quickly. (Potential newsletter article: How Staging Helped This House Sell in 30 Days.)

- × Feature: Mike's Flowers has amazing bouquets!

- ✓ Benefit: With hundreds of flowers and experienced designers, you'll delight your loved ones with flowers from Mike's that show how much you care. (Potential newsletter article: Beyond Traditional Flowers: New Looks for Your Table.)

See, it's all about them. Not you. It's a subtle difference—the same information, but phrased so that the emphasis is not on how great the product or service is...but what the product or service can do to make the customer's life better. Information they didn't know they needed—and might have had to pay to get somewhere else. Ask yourself: What does he or she care about? How can I provide it? And most important, how can I earn the customer's trust by showing them I'm looking out for them?

Imagine, for example, that you are a real estate agent. You believe that home ownership is one of the joys and rights of life, and that it is your duty to make sure that as many people as possible can enjoy owning a home, without the stress that can sometimes accompany the buying process. You then will work out ways to act this principle out, including:

- Providing educational materials on buying a home.
- Making sure your focus is on the client relationship and removing the stress and uncertainties of the process of buying a home.
- Finding ways to open up home ownership to as many people as possible by working with financing experts, and finding ways to convert renters into home owners.

So, to accomplish all that, you might:

- Fill your website with useful articles that educate your clients on these very ideas.
- Send out your newsletter on a regular basis, with articles that educate your clients and assure them you're in tune with their needs.
- Consider your clients' "stress points" in a real estate transaction and seek to minimize them, either by retooling your work processes and/or by finding partners to help. Then you could provide a "stress-proof guarantee" and show all the ways you'll make clients' lives easier.
- Ask financing experts to provide articles for your newsletter and website that educate clients about financing options.
- Use newsletters and social media to reach out to renters and other people who might benefit from owning a home.

Do you see how you can move from self-centered marketing of your features to focusing on the benefits that fill your clients' needs? And can you see now how much more attractive you become to your clients with this new position?

RULE #2: ESTABLISH EXPERTISE

These days, people are a bit at sea when they head out to buy something they need. They've done their research online. They've considered their options. But an increasing number are heading to a brick-and-mortar location so they can touch and feel the product and, hopefully, get some advice.

Here's where you—or your well-trained, customer-focused staff—come in. Who knows your product better than you? You are your customer's in-person expert. And study after study shows that people trust experts—even when they don't know anything about that person's actual credentials. To extrapolate, whether you are selling a product or a service, one of the best ways to establish a trusting relationship with customers is to stake out your area of expertise, then prove it.

It's not enough just to say you are an expert at real estate or insurance or whatever else is your passion. Lots of people say that. Instead, think hard about what you do that sets you apart from others. If you are in real estate, maybe you're the expert at real estate in a particular neighborhood, or you understand the needs of seniors or first-time buyers. Maybe your mortgage brokerage specializes in fast turnarounds, or refinancing. By carving out a smaller slice of the world, it's easier to become the number-one expert in that niche.

Say you want to make the claim you're an expert at (for example) financial planning for boomers. How to prove it? I think one of the best ways of offering proof is to share your expertise with others. It puts that proof in black-and-white, right there on the page or on the screen. So get your knowledge down on paper. Don't worry if your articles aren't New York Times-standard, just commit what you know to the page. Imagine you are talking with a client; simply write down what you would say. By creating a series of articles or reports or blog posts you are providing proof that you really are the expert you say you are. It's even OK to leave yourself open to possible naysayers—engaging with competing information can let you present the case for your side. Then, when a client chooses you, they feel you know the possible competitors…and are ready to prove you're better.

Finally, show what you've done for others; how your expertise works in the real world. To do that, gather case studies or testimonials from happy clients and share them with the world on your website or in print. If you have clients who have done what you said and gotten a good result, tell the world! You owe it to yourself—and to the customer who's going to be better off choosing you.

This is the system I use myself. I have determined I am an expert in using newsletters containing useful and thought-provoking information to build real, long-term relationships with clients (rather than as just another keep-in-touch tool); I share my expertise through newsletters, on my blog, in articles and videos, and now in this book. And I prove my success with testimonials and case studies on my website.

RULE #3: BE AUTHENTIC

Customers are a canny breed: they know the difference between when you're being sincere (I use the word "authentic") and when it's all about money. To build deep, lasting relationships with your customers there's really only one true strategy. Be authentic and true to yourself.

Over at Digiday.com (a virtual community for digital marketers and advertisers) I found a great collection of views on authenticity, 21st century-style. Do you agree? Do these ideas match your reality of when you choose what companies and providers to give your business to? Thinking about these quotes will go a long way to helping you find your own authenticity.

> Authentic means being transparent. We know our audience knows us well, and so we have to be honest.
>
> - Joe Barbagallo, social media manager, Volvo Cars U.S.

To us, being real means being honest, inclusive, boldly unapologetic, refreshingly to the point, insightful and occasionally, a little edgy. We steer clear of being artificial, judgmental, insecure, full of hot air, timid or gimmicky.

- Rick Maynard, senior manager of public relations, KFC Corp.

The original "idea" of authenticity was essentially a way for corporations to attempt to not sound corporate in their marketing efforts—or at the very least to stay true to their essence. Increasingly in the social age, it has come to mean a way for brands to be conversational, to be colloquial... more direct and everyday and friendly than perhaps you have been or you think your competition is.

- Kyle Sherwin, SVP Strategy, Accounts & Media, Arcade Creative Group, Sony Music

Back to you. How can you show you're a real person, with passions, real-world experience and—yes—humanity? How can you cut through all the bull and connect, just like we used to? How can you create relationships with your clients that actually mean something? A connection so genuine that people will seek you out and, maybe even pay extra for it? How can you share your Why?

CASE STUDY: JACK AND FRANK

Back in the 1940s, the story goes, Frank Sinatra asked his pal Jackie Gleason for a drink recommendation. The comedian told the crooner "Jack Daniel's," and a love affair was born. Sinatra kept a bottle onstage at his concerts, drank the whiskey in bars and casinos, and ordered it for the rest of the Rat Pack.

Matt Blevins, Senior Brand Manager for the Jack Daniel Distillery says, "It was one of those authentic relationships. We never paid him." (Bloomberg Businessweek 3/6/2014)

Jack Daniel's in 1940 was just another bottle on the shelf. With Sinatra's endorsement it became America's best-selling whiskey. And the endorsement was indeed authentic—on his death in 1998, Sinatra was buried with a flask of Jack Daniel's. So how does Jack Daniel's leverage this story? The Tennessee whiskey-maker recently released a $150, ninety-proof bottle of Sinatra Select whiskey—its most expensive bottle ever. It comes in a coffin-shaped box, accompanied by the booklet "A Timeless Story of Friendship", detailing the history of Frank and Jack.

For booklet, read "newsletter"—because newsletters aren't about format, they're about stories. And this is one heck of a story.

What makes this a great representation of the brand? It's a true story of a real relationship. It's authentic.

Your customers lead the same kind of busy life you lead. If you consider how you can make these customers' lives better—how you can be useful to them and provide them with a smile, a feeling of belonging, a new idea or an old one reinterpreted—then you'll win their trust. And their business. For this, you need to look into yourself and find out—not just your Why (the reason you get up in the morning) but what it is that makes you different from your competitors: Your unique selling proposition (USP). Once you've identified it, you need to get it out there. Stay tuned. In the next chapter, you'll read all about it.

THE TAKEAWAY

Keep your customers among the 21% who are satisfied with your service and will continue to do business with you by building trusting long-term relationships. Do this by putting customers first and by being authentic. And don't forget: It's not about you. It's about them.

THE EXERCISE

What does authentic mean to you?

Consider how (and if) you are reflecting the real you in your marketing?

Then look at your competitors' marketing. What are they doing right? Are they building trusting relationships with their customers?

Are you?

Don't forget—if you have comments or critiques (or compliments) send them along. If you have questions about authenticity or ideas on building relationships of trust, send them along. Best of all: If you've built strong bonds with your very own YRCs and YNCs, tell me how! I may use your company and idea as an example in my blog. Visit the book's website at **www.AlwaysConnectBook.com** to get in touch.

You, Your Customers And Your USP

CHAPTER 4

What's the magic "something" that makes you different from everyone else? Is it your high level of personal service? Your extensive knowledge of the local market? Your ability to figure out the best-selling advertising angle for any house? Whatever it is, that's your Unique Selling Proposition. Finding and using your USP is the most important thing you can do to market your business.

Your Unique Selling Proposition could be tied to your product, its price, the way you distribute it or the promotional strategy you use to get it out there. But what it actually boils down to is the following: Why should your ideal customer buy from you rather than any—or all—of your competitors?

WHAT MAKES THESE COMPANIES UNIQUE?

Flash Quiz! These slogans illustrate what make particular companies different from their competitors. Some you'll recognize immediately because they're classics (although maybe no longer used). Others are newer, or represent a rebranding initiative. And still others you may not recognize at all. See if you can put a brand name to each one. (Answers below)

- A complete workout in 30 minutes!
- Think fresh.
- The World's Best Egg
- When it absolutely, positively, has to be there overnight.
- It's the only light beer that's also a [BRAND].
- One for One.
- ...to leave the softest possible pawprint on our planet.
- The first interactive toothbrush. [1]

These companies found a niche in the market that wasn't being filled, or identified something consumers didn't like and made it right. Their USP's resonated strongly with customers, strongly enough to make that USP a key aspect of their brand. That helped the companies in their search for market share, and made many of them market leaders.

Let's look at some of them in more detail:

- Curves understood that busy women didn't have time to spend hours at the gym. They created an exercise circuit that gives women a good workout in half an hour.

- Subway realized that nobody wanted a dried-out, pre-made sandwich. They introduced made-to-order subs, built in front of the customer so you could see they were fresh.

- The Country Hen changed the perception that eggs are, well, just eggs. They told customers what made their company different from everyone else in a uniquely personal way—we'll discuss their story later in this chapter.

1 Answers: Curves; Subway; The Country Hen; FedEx; Corona Light; TOMS; The Cate & Levi Collection; Procter and Gamble/Oral-B

- When Corona introduced Corona Light, the ad campaign's tone implied "of course you know Corona is a good beer, so Corona Light must be the best light beer, because it has the quality of Corona". This USP is also extra-unique: No other beer brand is going to say "Our light beer is as good as a Corona."

- The owners of TOMS were passionate about reducing third-world poverty, and built the company's reputation by sending one pair of shoes to third-world children for every pair purchased. While the actual shoe exchange has its detractors, the USP of "do good by wearing our shoes" has been a strong draw for those who believe in the TOMS mission.

- Josh Title, founder of the Cate & Levi Collection, saw a gap in the market—wouldn't adults who valued organic, environmentally-responsible products want the same for their children? He filled a then-gap in the market for stuffed toys and other soft décor and play items for children that are one-of-a-kind, safe, and beautiful to look at. His "pawprint" was soft. And profitable.

- Procter & Gamble Co. announced recently it was introducing the world's first interactive toothbrush, to make brushing your teeth "smarter and more personal." The company's Oral B electric toothbrush uses Bluetooth technology to work with a smartphone app that will personalize brushing settings.

P&G are a particularly interesting example—they're the current winner in what I like to call "The Toothbrush Wars," with a number of toothbrush manufacturers fighting tooth and nail (so to speak) for the leading market position in this lucrative business. Their weapons? Their Unique Selling Propositions.

The world of dueling USPs can be a tricky one. There must be 50 different kinds of toothbrushes out there, each offering something different: bristles that change color, easy-grip handles, special shapes, interactivity. It's a sea of USPs out there in toothbrush-land!

Ironically, this tsunami of USPs actually encourages customers to switch brands to the one with the latest gimmick. Fortunately for small-business owners, most of your competition doesn't have a marketing department working on identifying—and selling—their USP. You've got a head start.

THE EULOGY QUESTION

Everyone, and I mean everyone, has their own Unique Selling Proposition—you just have to find it and get it out there. And I'm here to help you do that. Pinpointing the factor that makes you different from everyone else requires some in-depth soul-searching, but it will pay you dividends to spend some time thinking about your own special USP. Your creativity may have been sparked by reading other companies' USPs, and the exercise at the end of this chapter will help you take the next steps.

But in the meantime, here's a taste of that exercise: The Eulogy Question. The vice president of strategy and marketing for Edison Research, Tom Webster, came up with what he calls, "the single best question you can ask your customers."

If [my company] were to die, what would you miss?

Webster's question goes right to the heart of your company—its USP. What do you do that is so important to your customers that if you stopped doing it, they would miss it?

What I mean is, it's probably not all that memorable to say you're an expert at real estate or insurance or whatever else is your passion. Lots of people say that. Instead, consider your company's "eulogy question." What do you think your customers would miss? For example, if you were a real estate agent specializing in rural properties, would a buyer interested in purchasing a farm miss your expertise in septic systems and wells? Your knowledge of zoning restrictions? You bet they would.

So one way to differentiate yourself is by carving out a small slice of the world and becoming the number-one expert in that niche. Clients who need that expertise will beat a path to your door.

A REAL ESTATE EXAMPLE

Real estate agents and brokers make up a large proportion of my newsletter business. There's a lot of agents—it's a tough business—but each one can succeed dramatically by finding his or her Unique Selling Proposition and getting it out there.

So what's Unique? A real estate agent can't really differentiate him- or herself in terms of product; they all sell houses, land, condos and commercial buildings, etc. And while some real estate agents do see their USPs as price-related and lower their commissions to get new business, this strategy might not hold up in the long run.

But how about this?

Case Study: The Seniors' Agent

A real estate agent based in Florida realized that seniors represented a large and wealthy segment of the market for real estate. Empty-nesters looking to downsize and snowbirds wanting to relocate, usually to a smaller place than they had up north. The agent enjoyed the rewards of working with seniors, and he genuinely wanted to see them have the best possible experience buying, moving, and settling in.

He carved out a niche helping seniors downsize, including taking special courses in his field to gain credentials with a specialist designation. Now he doesn't just sell houses, he connects older homebuyers to the wide variety of services they needed to make the move to a smaller home, often in a state or city new to them.

Matching his clients with lawyers, estate planners, stagers, auction houses and organizers, he's made himself an indispensible part of the life-stage-transition process—someone that newly-settled customers recommend whole-heartedly to their friends as "the guy who helped us feel like this is our new home."

Now that's a Unique Selling Proposition.

This has worked for many real estate agents. They've gained a large share of a lucrative niche market, and they've helped thousands of seniors by making it easier to navigate that transition from family home to retirement pad.

As I mentioned, I help many of my clients find their Unique Selling Propositions, because it can be a pretty daunting task. It's even more daunting trying to figure out how to get it out there, so it helps to have someone else's informed perspective.

Some of my clients are fortunate enough to have a great story to tell; they found their USPs and their voices simultaneously. They've opted to explain "Why I'm different" in a compelling way, with stories that engage and delight their customers. One of the best ways to get this story out there is through newsletters.

Here's a great example of a fun, unique story, told via a funky newsletter that has made the company a market leader in its territory.

CASE STUDY: THE COUNTRY HEN

I've mentioned The Country Hen before ("The World's Best Egg"); the company is an egg producer in Maine. They're not a client, but I wish they had been! The Country Hen distributes a regular newsletter every four to six weeks with each six-pack of eggs. This newsletter—and the stories it tells—plays a significant role in positioning the company. And it works really, really well!

Owner George Bass started The Country Hen in 1988. His was a unique approach to egg farming. It was the first organic Omega-3 egg farm in the USA. He believed that only the happiest, healthiest hens would produce The World's Best Egg—which is what he was selling. (Notice he's willing to declare his "expert" status right up front!)

His hens roamed freely through spacious, sunlit barns with porches that protected them while still allowing them access to the outdoors. They ate specially-formulated food made onsite. When selling

> the product, George ensured the eggs were fresh by packaging them in six-packs and only shipping 15 dozen at a time to stores.
>
> Millions of eggs later, he still does.
>
> George wanted customers to feel a strong connection to the company. Using an appealing, folksy style, the newsletters include nutritional information but also amateurish (but delightful) photos of animals, recipes and fun farm stories, as well as hot farm topics in the news (such as ethanol), farm poetry, customer letters, etc.
>
> Customers loved his sometimes-rambling personal voice, and they loved the newsletter that felt like a letter from a friend. Nearly 150 customers a year visit the farming operation to see where their eggs come from. Almost 900 of them wrote in to name The Country Hen's new baby goat (the name "Dulci" won).
>
> These customers and thousands more propelled the company to the top of its industry.
>
> In regular cost-benefit analyses, The Country Hen revisits whether the newsletter still works and what effects it has, but according to the sales department: "the discontinuation of the newsletters was never a consideration because of its obvious success and appeal with our customers. The success of this program was obvious in less than three weeks' time," thanks to a deluge of emails, letters, and calls from customers opening their egg cartons and enjoying The Country Hen's newsletter.

The Country Hen explained why it was different from its competitors by telling stories and sharing pictures in a fun way through a useful, interesting newsletter. It worked magic for them. Would it work for you?

THE TAKEAWAY

In this chapter, we've looked at your Unique Selling Proposition—the one thing that makes you, your product or your service different from anyone else's. And we've discussed how to share that USP by positioning yourself as an expert and passing on your knowledge.

EXERCISE

- Step #1: You've already taken this first step by raising your awareness of other companies' USPs through the quiz.
- Step # 2: Look at your competitors' marketing materials and see if you can find their USPs.
- Step #3: Put yourself in your clients' shoes and ask yourself the Eulogy Question: What would your customers miss if your company died?
- Step #4: Ask the same question of your most loyal customers. Is there a disconnect between their answers and what you thought they'd say? If so, reconcile it, bearing in mind it's about the customer's wants and needs, not yours.
- Step #5: This is the hard part. Step outside yourself and consider a whole range of ideas that relate to your products or services: What little thing do you do that identifies you as something different and that will stick in people's minds? Maybe wrapping your product in brown paper instead of the ubiquitous plastic bags? Or taking herbs when you

distribute your newsletter, as the real estate agent in Chapter One did?

- Step #6: Connect all these dots, and chances are you have your USP.

If you're lucky and creative enough to want to roll out your story—and if you know how and where to get it out—it could take you where you want to go. But I'm here to tell you that you don't need a story to make a compelling, useful and interesting newsletter (with a big dash of personality) that your clients will want to hold on to… sometimes for months.

That's where we'll go in Chapter Five.

Don't forget to send me your comments and ideas. If you have questions about your USP or want to try out a story on me, by all means do—visit **www.AlwaysConnectBook.com**

PART 2

Content Marketing

CHAPTER 5

As I said in the Introduction, I'm all about newsletters. They allow you to create real relationships with your leads and customers—but without shaking hands with each of them individually. They increase your referrals and position you as a trusted expert, not a salesperson. By the time you finish reading this book (if not before) my hope is that you'll be excited about newsletters, too.

Here's where the rubber hits the road. In the next three chapters, I'll be giving you detailed instructions on how to plan an effective newsletter, and what to put in it. My goal is to make this whole newsletter-creation process simpler than you can imagine so you don't feel bogged down and overwhelmed. I don't want you to view birthing a newsletter—and continuing its publication—as merely another item on your to-do list. Throughout the week you will soon be thinking, "I am so going to add that to my next newsletter!" and taking calls from people who fell in love with you through your latest newsletter.

Every company needs a newsletter—even need-based businesses such as a funeral home or assisted-living facility; businesses people don't need right now, but will sometime in the future. Because newsletters build trust, and trust is at a premium these days, planting the seeds of long-term customer growth with your newsletter is crucial. Maybe someone opens your newsletter to read an article that sparked their interest, then thinks 'Hmm, this is interesting, although I don't need this service... I don't even want to think about that right now.' But the next evening he or she could be at a cocktail party with someone who is handling the needs of an elderly family member. Now you're fresh in their mind as a business to refer, as someone to be trusted to tell their friends about.

That's where we get into Big, Maybe Exponential Growth. It's not just the power of your newsletter. It's the power of reaching the friends and family of everyone who reads your newsletter. Of being trusted by your readers, and then endorsed by them when they say "Check out Jane Doe—she seems to really know what she's talking about."

There's a great report that came out last year on "content marketing." The Content Marketing Institute defines content marketing as "the art of communicating with your customers and prospects without selling." It's also "non-interruption marketing."

What does this mean exactly? "Instead of pitching your products or services, you are delivering information that makes your buyer more informed. The essence of this content strategy is the belief that if we, as businesses, deliver consistent, ongoing valuable information to buyers, they ultimately reward us with their business and loyalty."

Content marketing certainly encompasses the value of what we're talking about here—developing useful, interesting content for customers to encourage them to act in a particular way. The report, by Demand Gen, includes good news about content marketing: 71.6% of survey respondents said they "place a higher emphasis on the trustworthiness" of the content they view. And 92.6% were willing to consider business-developed content (such as your newsletter) trustworthy.

As you know, these days people are more apt to rely on experts to tell them what to do. Your newsletter represents a "non-interruptive" way to help them solve problems. Consistently, and over time, articles build on articles and advice on advice, eventually building a library of knowledge. Soon, your status as the go-to-expert is firmly established, simply by penning a few newsletters.

Newsletters help you easily keep in touch with Your Repeat Customers. Instead of cranking out a personal email to each past customer, you can add them to your mailing list. Send them your regular newsletters with information that makes their lives better, and they'll be itching to buy from you again. Your newsletter enables you to share your passion—which I assume is about making your life and your customers' lives more fulfilling, a theme most entrepreneurs share.

YES, EVEN FUNERAL HOMES

Eyebrows are always raised when I declare that, yes, even funeral homes need newsletters. What, for heaven's sake (no pun intended), can a funeral home put in a newsletter? Why would they need one? Would someone read the catchy, colorful copy and think, 'Hey, I'd really like to hire this funeral home to make my life better!"? Probably not. But, as I stated earlier, newsletters are about planting seeds. Eventually you want a garden full of potential clients. Isn't it true that everyone will plan a funeral sometime in his or her life?

CASE STUDY: LIFE BEFORE DEATH

In a small town there are two funeral homes. Let's call them Dyer and Co. and Restinpeez Brothers, Inc. They're both good. Indeed, they share business in town fifty-fifty.

Townspeople usually choose one or the other based on family tradition. But Restinpeez Brothers, Inc. wants more business—without having to open up a second establishment in another town. Inflating demand is out (killing people is wrong), so they must take business away from Dyer.

Here's how a newsletter-based strategy would work:

Restinpeez would actively position itself as the hub of the community. A funeral home is well-connected with a small town's residents already, so it's a natural step to further develop those ties. They'd start producing a monthly newsletter that serves the community. Announcements of local events, "good news"

> stories of awards, achievements and good deeds done, useful information to help new residents settle in, a way for people to include their own stories of life in the community, and plenty of articles that help people live life to the fullest in their own home town. The newsletter would be distributed free to "nodes" within the town—places where people hang out. Laundromats, diners, barbershops, even the dentist's waiting room. People could also subscribe to the newsletter and receive it (for free) in the mail or by email. Over time, Restinpeez's newsletter could become almost a mini-newspaper—one serving the community at a grassroots level. Their now-locally-famous newsletter regularly touches the community with useful, entertaining, interesting information. Information that helps people live their lives better. What it doesn't talk about is death or dying. Restinpeez might be in the business of death, but their newsletter will be about life.
>
> This effort to integrate the Restinpeez business into the community can lead to them becoming the funeral home of choice... to Restinpeez Brothers taking business from Dyer, as many residents, both long-timers and new arrivals (who feel welcomed to the community by Restinpeez's newsletter) opt to use "the company with the newsletter."

As you can see, most businesses—even funeral homes—need a newsletter to capture and retain customers. It's simply an extension of your sales and marketing plans, after all. But before you design your first newsletter, begin with a plan. The more you clarify up front about your target client and the voice you wish to adopt, the easier the newsletter-writing process will be.

Ready to plan? Let's walk through six steps to figure out how you want to use your newsletter.

STEP #1: WHAT DO YOU WANT TO ACHIEVE?

In order to boost business, Restinpeez went after a larger market share. A local real-estate company may want to establish its agents as go-to experts—on more than just houses—in a particular neighborhood. Maybe an agent can write an article about the best pizza-delivery services or a beautiful trail to hike with your dog. This helps provide credibility: not only can this company's agents sell you the perfect house, they'll help you integrate into your new community.

What you want to achieve by publishing your own newsletter will ultimately depend on your business niche, your challenges and goals, and your market position. You'll use your newly formed newsletter to build trusting relationships, but there are many ways newsletters can help achieve your goals.

- Gently market yourself to your clients as a trusted advisor, not a pushy salesperson.
- Encourage customers to take action on a purchase they're considering.
- Warm up prospects by showing them how your tips have benefited others.
- Build your reputation as a go-to expert.
- Keep in touch with your local area or business territory and their immediate concerns.
- Take business from a competitor.
- Maintain your customer base with regular communication.

After each of our six steps—like the one above—I'll ask you to write down your thoughts. Some steps will ask you to answer questions. Others, like the list above, will involve some hard, out-of-the-box thinking. What works for you and what makes you want to run for the hills? Gauge your comfort level as you read through a list such as this. Once you've read all the steps and jotted down your answers and thoughts you now have a plan to create your own newsletter!

Write what you want to achieve here. Be as specific as you can. The more exact your goal, the more likely you are to meet it. For example, "I want to expand my business" doesn't give you much to go on (how? to whom?). But what if you reworded it as "I want to increase business income by 25 percent over the next nine months, by attracting customers who spend more than my current clientele"?

MY GOAL IS:

____

____

____

____

____

STEP #2: YOUR TARGET AUDIENCE

Before you can create a newsletter, you need to know who your typical customers or prospects are. This could include some or all of the answers to the questions below.

- How old are they?
- What education level have they achieved?
- What type of home/business do they have?
- Do they have a family?
- How much disposable income do they have?
- What do they do during their leisure time?
- Where do they vacation?
- What are their interests? What are they really passionate about?
- What are their greatest hopes and fears?
- What keeps them up at night? (This last one is very important—it's the key to creating a newsletter they will devour.)

DESCRIBE YOUR TYPICAL CUSTOMERS HERE:

____

____

____

____

STEP #3: HOW DO YOU WANT TO HELP THEM?

Look back to your Unique Selling Proposition and re-acquaint yourself with what you can give to your customers that is viewed as special. Are you stuck? Consider these examples.

- What information can you provide to help make the right decisions about products to potentially purchase?
- What you can tell them about your field, region, or product that's truly something new—something that will make them go "wow!" (Although you might have to dig a little to answer this, be patient: nailing the answer is pure gold.)
- Can you provide information that helps them realize their dreams?
- Can you provide information that allays fears and instead solves problems?
- Can you provide information that feeds their passions?

Yes, you can. Believe me, you can. Now, write notes about how you can make your customers' lives better here. Don't neglect the small things.

I CAN MAKE MY CUSTOMERS' LIVES BETTER WITH/BY:

____

____

____

STEP #4: HOW SHOULD YOUR NEWSLETTER SOUND?

One of your jobs as a business owner is to monitor competitors' advertising material—such as their websites, social-media sites, special offers, television and magazine ads. You've probably been looking for quite some time at your competition's customer communications before you sit down to draft your first newsletter. Maybe without even realizing it, you've also been learning what works and what doesn't, as if you were a potential customer. Sorting out what you like and don't like about their material can help you determine the tone you want to give your newsletter. Even just knowing what you don't want to be is incredibly useful!

Here are some ways to start thinking about the "voice" of your newsletter.

First of all, the newsletter should be a seamless extension of your business. Because you strive to give personal, professional service or sell quality products, your newsletter must reflect that professionalism, and quality, or the feeling you hope your customers get when they've just experienced doing business with you. If you're a bubbly stylist, or a serious financial analyst, or a cheerful and determined real estate agent, your newsletter should reflect your true self, and the tone in which you normally enjoy doing business. Is it formal or informal? Straightforward and shoot-from-the-hip, or mellow and laid-back?

Do you want to include humour? (Remember the real-estate agent who included his daughter's joke, and the customer who missed it when it wasn't included?) What about community news and stories?

How should it reflect your goal? If your goal is to become the go-to expert, should the newsletter be useful and matter-of-fact? Or do you want it to be a mixture of solid advice and lighter content, with a call to action such as setting up a meeting with you?

Do you want to encourage a dialogue with customers through your newsletter? If so, strive to be interactive with quizzes, contests and opportunities for readers to get involved, maybe the "letter to the editor" approach. (As The Country Hen's newsletter, mentioned in Chapter 4, does so well!)

Do you want to "go naked?" People choose to do business with real people, so how do you reflect the real–authentic–you? List your personality traits–good and bad–and circle the ones you want to share. Are you engaging and charismatic? Then include your picture in your newsletter. Are you proud of your family's involvement in your business? Include them, too. How about a fun candid snap of your dog or cat? Yes, people like to see the fluffy side of you, the authentic person they want to hear from.

Do you want to share your passion about what it is you do? Tell stories. Lots of them. Perhaps case studies or testimonials from happy clients (with their permission, of course). If you have clients who have taken your advice to heart or used your services and gotten great results, you owe it to yourself and others to share this.

Do you want to deeply involve your customers in your business? Bring them inside the circle. Give them an opportunity to comment on what you've done and what you're planning. You'll no doubt receive good feedback you can use to improve your product or service—for free—as well as helping your clients feel like they have an interest in your business doing well.

It's humanizing for people to hear that you're not perfect. After all, they're not either. So if you have a story to share about a mistake you've made, don't hold back. Just be sure to stress that you have learned from those mistakes!

You can also tell people about the good stuff you do. Maybe it has nothing to do with your business but everything about how much you love your community. Do you coach little-league games? Volunteer at local food pantry?

Finally, personality is important, but it's vital to do it well. Write with integrity. Don't be someone other than the real you. And don't overdo it. Remember that people are ultimately interested in their own lives, not the minute details of yours. Now write down—in just a few words—what you want the tone of your newsletter to be.

MY NEWSLETTER'S TONE SHOULD BE:

____

____

STEP #5: HOW SHOULD YOUR NEWSLETTER LOOK?

Do you want it to be a one-pager with interesting copy flowing on both sides? Or do you need more space, such as a tiny booklet of less than 10 pages? If your newsletter is more frequent, go small. If you plan to include a lot of testimonials or case studies, you'll need more space.

Do you want to print it or email it? There are pros and cons of both—we'll evaluate these two options in more depth in a later chapter. For now, just note what means you'd like to use. Don't worry about cost or the logistics. I'll walk you through each process, including tech issues that might arise or how the heck you'll deliver to all the nodes around town.

What will you name it? Is the title quirky, funny or straight-to-the-point? The chosen name should reflect your business, your goal and the tone you've decided to adopt. Also consider your audience—if it's for customers with families then you may want to give your newsletter a warm, fuzzy name.

If you're a service company, opt for a community-focused name—"Springfield News & Views" or "Riverview Neighborhood Report." Don't stress too much about the "right" name. The fundamental value is in the content and the services you'll eventually provide.

Write down your thoughts on what you want your newsletter to look like (even sketch a rough layout!).

MY NEWSLETTER WILL LOOK LIKE:

____

____

____

____

____

STEP #6: OTHER STUFF THAT'S IMPORTANT

It's essential you publish your newsletter regularly so clients become accustomed to receiving it. Taking six months off isn't doing anybody any favors. Think of all those missed opportunities to engage customers! Decide whether you will publish monthly or every two months, and on what day of the month. Remember that everything takes more time than you expect. For a monthly newsletter, count on at least a week for printing (unless you're e-mailing it) and an additional two weeks for mailing. We'll discuss scheduling later: I'll even give you two useful templates.

Decide on a budget—and vow to stick to it. Consider that a lot of this newsletter's creation will be your own time (unless you have employees with superb writing or design skills, or a burning desire to help, while still fulfilling their job roles). If an employee has some design skills and the ability to write, great, just ensure he or she has a full understanding of the message you wish to convey. You definitely don't want to halt production after the first issue due to a pressing need to revamp the whole thing, all based on a misunderstanding.

Handing the newsletter off to someone else doesn't mean shedding your involvement. You still need to meet with that employee well before the newsletter is scheduled to decide what will go in it. Check back in part way through the publishing timeline to make sure it's going along as it should. And no matter how busy you are, or how much you trust this employee, make sure you see the newsletter before it goes to press. Consider running it by another person you trust, someone very detail-oriented, to catch any typos. It's very hard for a writer to spot their own typos!

Below, write how often you want to publish the newsletter and what resources are available. Consider the cost of time: yours and anyone else you involve in producing it. If you are lucky enough to hand over the newsletter to a good staff person, don't bury him or her in other work; you're adding a responsibility—consider easing up on other parts of that person's workload.

MY SCHEDULE WILL BE:

____

THE TAKEAWAY

If you've jotted down your answers and thoughts for the six steps in this chapter, you now have a plan to create your own newsletter!

Publishing your own newsletter isn't rocket science, but you do want to be sure it looks—and sounds—consistent and professional. After all, it reflects you and your business. This is your calling card, something that reflects you and your business, so do it well. This is an investment in the future of your business, and the customers you'll gain will more than recoup this cost. Remember, many things in life, from a kitchen remodel to birthing a newsletter, take more time and more money than you expect.

In the next two chapters, I'll provide information on content: What is content? Why is it important to stick to The Golden Rules of Newsletter Publishing? How do I produce useful, interesting and informative content that will make my customers' lives easier—and make them love me for it?

I'll also provide information on alternatives to this DIY approach to newsletter publishing. These include hiring a writer or team of writers, farming out production and distribution, and even buying template newsletters that you can personalize in all sorts of ways.

THE EXERCISE

Good news—You've already completed this chapter's series of exercises!

See? It didn't hurt a bit.

AND…

Remember to find me at **www.AlwaysConnectBook.com**. If you have any questions or comments, or want to provide good examples of things you've done right (or even things you've done wrong) with your customer communications, send them along. You never know, I may include them in future editions of this book.

The Golden Rules Of Newsletter Content

CHAPTER 6

Paul Lemberg—a business and marketing coach whom I've mentioned earlier in this book—is a great content guy. So what's his perspective on newsletters? Read on to find out. I guarantee you'll be surprised.

> Most newsletters are filled with self-serving drivel about the company. Who cares about employee promotions, or that you just had a wonderful company picnic? Boring! Instead, fill your newsletter with stimulating ideas, case studies and practical tips that add value to your customers and help them do better business too, no matter their industry.
>
> - Paul Lemberg, Business and Marketing Coach

Why not tell us what you really think, Paul? Actually, though, he's absolutely right[1]. Here's my take on what not to put in a newsletter. Consider this very likely scenario as a customer receives a newsletter.

1 http://www.businessknowhow.com/marketing/customer-loyalty.htm

> Customer: Ding! Hey! New email. Ooh, a newsletter! I like those!
>
> Oh, wait. It's from a software company. A letter from the CEO, no less.

And that's where things start to go wrong, terribly wrong. Let me give you a quote from the lead story, Our New Corporate Strategy: *"We have established a new corporate strategy designed to meet the continuously evolving needs of the marketplace and enable our customers to achieve success."*

Here's some info to be found in a secondary story, Aligning Our Structure to the Strategy: *"We are re-aligning our business units to have their full attention and focus on product development."*

And when the CEO signs off: *"We believe it is important that our customers and business partners have a clear picture of where [company name] is headed in the future. We appreciate your business and look forward to helping you achieve great success in the world of digital media."*

Are you eager to know more about their 'business units'? Yeah, right! You—and most other people—would have skipped to the next email in their inbox or tossed this newsletter into the recycling bin.

After reading the last five chapters, can you figure out what this company did wrong in its newsletter? What might have caused people to chuck it and move on? (Not to worry, I'll tell you.)

To begin with, the focus in this newsletter is erroneously on the company, not the customer. Although the company believes that changes within the company will benefit the customer, the content of the message is about *us, us, us*. Not *you, you, you*. Very one-sided, right? So the customer is left wondering if there is even a space for him or her in the company's culture. He feels lectured. Alienation is definitely not the feeling you want to impress upon readers!

Second, it fails the "so what?" test. Do customers really care about the company's new hires and new corporate structure? Probably not. This kind of news is more relevant internally and doesn't need to be broadcast outside of the company. And certainly not when the newsletter has already failed at showing that they are focused on the customer. (Now, if the new hire was an expert with something to share with the reader…)

Finally, that newsletter is boring with a capital B. People are busy. They want to be informed and entertained. Reading a newsletter should be fun, engaging and easy! They don't have the time (or the desire) to read something that appears dull and not particularly helpful or relevant to them at the moment.

You know what it's like to be cornered at a party by someone who won't stop talking about their job, their kids or their hobby? The unfortunate newsletter above is a printed version of that cocktail-party snore. And, please, please, please don't be boring. Become a cure for boredom instead!

Golden Rule #1 of Newsletter Publishing:

Make your newsletters for and about your customers. Respect their time and meet their needs.

Golden Rule #2 of Newsletter Publishing:

You must provide value—offer only information and articles that your customers find useful or entertaining.

I guarantee that any large or small company that does all of this consistently and well will succeed in attracting and retaining customers.

CONTENT OVERVIEW

Remember back in Chapter Five, the idea of "content"? A quick flashback:

Instead of pitching your products or services, you are delivering information that makes your buyer more informed. The essence of this content strategy is the belief that if we, as businesses, deliver consistent, ongoing valuable information to buyers, they ultimately reward us with their business and loyalty.

"Content" is marketer-speak for "articles and information." A good newsletter contains content that is different—your articles are not the same blah-blah-blah drivel that your competitors include in their marketing materials. These articles should be "must-reads" for your clients, with information that isn't easily available elsewhere. Strive to publish content that people will want to share on Facebook, clip out for a colleague, or stick on the company bulletin board. You want your readers to say, "Hey Jane, I just read this article that might solve your problem!"

A good newsletter also contains content that is new. If people have already heard what you have to say, they'll stop reading, no matter what brilliant article is on the next page. They will be over and done with your newsletter if they feel they've 'already heard it'—and not just this particular newsletter but all future editions of your newsletter, too. So set your sights on putting out a piece of entertainment. Go big and go bold. Don't be afraid to be sensational. Throw a few head-scratchers in there—what I like to call the contrarian's point of view. Give readers the unexpected. Make them think a little. Maybe a story documenting what NOT to do in a situation, as opposed to a list of advice on what to do (yawn). Create the type of content your readers simply can't find anywhere else.

While most of your competitors' snoozeletters are boring people with articles like "10 Things You Already Know" and "Five Ways to State the Obvious," you will write content that makes people think, stuff that makes them go "huh?" In other words: Engage them and interest them at the same time.

Chances are your customers aren't a homogenous group. People have many different needs and wants. To complicate your task further, these needs and wants change every week—not everyone will respond to everything, and not everyone will choose your product or service. So use a variety of articles. Mix it up. Share links and first paragraphs of interesting articles you've stumbled across online, and fold in tips related to your business.

In the next chapter I've included sources of inspiration for writing intelligent, useful articles that not only engage your customers, but make them look forward to hearing from you.

CALL YOUR READERS TO ACTION

Give them a call to action—and now, not later. If your newsletter is going to work—in other words, increase your income or your new customers—you've got to find a way to encourage people to contact you and eventually become your client, perhaps multiple times. It's having lots of great content that will get readers hanging on your every word, but that's not worth squat if once they've read your articles, they don't take action. It's only by putting an offer into your newsletter that you'll get a return on your efforts. And it should be immediate! If readers wait, it's likely they'll do nothing.

The key to making effective calls to action is to introduce offers frequently enough that customers look forward to them, but not so often that they know when to expect them. (You may not want them waiting a month to buy your product or service because they expect you'll have a coupon coming up.)

Including a different offer each month can help you track the effectiveness of your newsletter—you'll easily see who comes in bearing each coupon, or who responds to a call to action..

The key to a good offer:

Present to your reader a reason why they should purchase from you today.

Let's go through that sentence in more detail.

"PRESENT TO YOUR READER..."

It's important to make it clear to your reader you are making them an offer.

- Include a physical or print-out coupon which they must bring to your business or make a purchase in order to get something. Discounts, free bonus gifts, free consultations and two-for-one deals are all great!
- Write an article in your newsletter that presents your offer, such as "How You Can Get a 10% Discount This Month." Make sure the article focuses on the benefits to your client rather than the features of your business (see features vs. benefits in Chapter Three)
- If you're using a case study, customer story or real-world example, including a paragraph with an offer at the end of the article: "If you'd like to achieve the results Bob did, visit us this month and receive a 10% discount for trying our service." (Offers don't have to be price-related, of course, just something that has value to the reader.)

"...A REASON WHY THEY SHOULD PURCHASE..."

This is one of the most powerful concepts in marketing. If you give a good reason why you are presenting an offer, people are much more likely to comply.

Dr. Robert Cialdini, in his book Influence: The Psychology of Persuasion, describes a study involving people lining up to use a photocopier.

In the study, someone tries to cut to the front of the line, testing the response to three requests:

Excuse me. I only have five pages. May I jump ahead?

60 percent of the line-waiters let her go ahead with this request.

Excuse me. I only have five pages. May I use the copy machine because I'm in a rush?

In this case, 94 percent let the person cut in!

Excuse me. I only have five pages. May I use the copy machine because I have to make some copies?

This statement got a similar response to the second one—93 percent of the time, the would-be copier was allowed to the front of the line.

There are two important concepts here:

If you give a reason, you are more likely to get what you want.

It really doesn't matter what that reason is. After all, the third sentence didn't give a 'real' reason at all. But still, almost everyone responded to her call to action.

She didn't just push ahead. She gave a reason. So why not put a reason into your offer, like:

- This is a new service I'm offering, and I want as many people to try it as possible.
- I'd like you to take up this offer, because I think it's the best deal in town right now.
- This is the once-a-year sale, so act now!

"...FROM YOU..."

This is where you clearly differentiate why you and your offer are better than the alternatives:

- It's the lowest priced on the market right now.
- We offer a lifetime guarantee.
- This is the only product to contain 100% hardwood.
- This is the only product to have been tested by 500 people in 20 countries.
- I'll also give you two free hours of consulting if you take me up on this offer.

"...TODAY"

Deadlines are important to get people to take action. Otherwise, there's a danger they will put your newsletter away and forget about you...and your product or service. Put some urgency in your offer:

- This offer is only available during the month of January.
- Consultations are only available this week before another project begins November 12.
- I can't afford to make this offer forever, so bring in your coupon before February 28.

The offer or call to action is an essential element of your newsletter. It's what makes it not just valuable and relevant to your readers, but what initiates doing business with them. Include one or more offers every month, tied as closely as possible to your newsletter's content.

THE TAKEAWAY

Choose your content carefully. If you make it all about the customer, if you make it useful, and you include a legitimately valuable offer, your customers will come…and you'll make money.

In the next chapter we'll start looking at how to get ideas for great content, and some simple templates to get you started.

THE EXERCISE

Write and schedule your offers for the year. Don't make them all coupons or Buy One Get One (BOGOs); think outside the box.

AND:

As you work through your newsletter plan, keep those cards and letters coming. I'm guessing that you're really coming up with some amazing ideas! I'd love to hear them. Get in touch at **www.AlwaysConnectBook.com**

GRAPHOPHOBICS TAKE NOTE

CHAPTER 7

Are you intimidated by the blank page—or the empty screen? You may suffer from graphophobia. That's right—the fear of writing or handwriting. The word comes from the Greek *grapho*, to write or draw, and of course *phobia* for fear.

Maybe you're thinking, "I wouldn't call it a phobia—I just don't like doing it!" and you're not alone! For many people, writing a newsletter ranks down there with going to the dentist, washing the car and clearing out the gutters. Emotionally painful tasks that are often the result of extreme procrastination. In other words, a royal pain!

But if you're going to continue publishing your newsletter, growing your audience and your income as you do, you simply can't view it that way. I challenge you to think of publishing your newsletter as fun and stimulating. We're going to look at how to make writing your newsletter a little—or a lot—less of a chore. I'm here to help with techniques and templates to make writing your newsletter easy, and dare I say it—fun?

CASE STUDY: CONQUERING GRAPHOPHOBIA

I had lunch the other week with a friend—this time we were meeting to talk business. She thought a newsletter would help one of her non-profit clients communicate more effectively with its donors. A good idea, I thought.

Although my friend was super-excited about launching a newsletter, she was daunted by the prospect of designing it, finding pictures, writing headlines, making sure everything lined up and looked pretty. All those little details that could turn into a full-time job—and that's not even including actually writing the articles. Understandably, she'd procrastinated. For months!.

This is what I told her:

It's not about the format, it's what you say. The best newsletters are authentic communications between a business owner (or charity director, in her case) and readers. They're about sharing information, and most importantly, sharing the passion that brought the charity and the donors together in the first place.

I suggested she write a heartfelt letter from the charity's directors, telling donors how their support had changed the lives of the children who benefited. Illustrate the letter with stories told by the children themselves, and she'd have a newsletter. Suddenly she saw the newsletter not as a project, but a mission-driven tale that was very easy to tell.

Last week, I received a draft of her newsletter, written on two pages of letter-sized paper in Arial font. It was a triumph. Each article succeeded in sharing the charity director's passion and enthusiasm. It was an authentic, honest communication. It was a successful newsletter.

SOME GENERAL RULES OF WRITING

People who come from a journalism or English-major background have an advantage—they're less likely to suffer from graphophobia, and they probably have a sense of writing structure and format. On the other hand, they're more likely to self-judge and worry about writing "perfect" copy. But never fear—whether you're a confident author or a nervous newbie, here are a few simple guidelines that will have you writing like a champ:

- Don't put too much pressure on yourself: Your newsletter doesn't have to be The New York Times. The most important thing is to express your ideas and your personality. In the example above, my friend was able to get across exactly what she wanted to say without worrying about layout, pictures or headlines, and it worked wonderfully!

- In fact, my advice is don't worry about format while you're writing. Pop open a Word document or your Google Docs and start your article. Just be yourself and type as fast as you can. You can go back and edit later. The point is to get the heart of the message onto the page. Handle the technical logistics later, instead of getting bogged down by wondering what it will look like on the page.

- That also means your writing shouldn't get in the way of what you're trying to say. Be clear, concise and use familiar language. Don't worry about style—the best newsletter writing is a relaxed tone, close to how you normally speak. Don't stress over grammar unless your business is word- or copy-focused (though do proofread for spelling errors, which can make you look sloppy).

- Collect ideas as you go along: If you try to come up with all your ideas on "Newsletter Day" you're asking your perhaps-already-tired brain for a sudden burst of creativity. Not easy. And probably not going to happen. Instead, build the habit of writing down newsletter ideas when they occur. Collect them in a specific place so they don't get lost. (Go ahead and jot down ideas on a napkin or the back of a receipt if that's what you have—just be sure you transfer them to your newsletter folder or list.) I use my cellphone to note ideas anywhere and everywhere, because I'm always carrying it.

- You might start small. That's okay. Any movement takes time to build a buzz. Your main task as a newsletter writer is to accumulate readers. Each issue should generate more and more readers. Starting with a small mailing list helps you get your footing without the pressure of a huge audience. As your numbers grow, so will your confidence and skill in making a great newsletter.

- Look for ways to write as you speak. If you're a better talker than writer, record yourself and then transcribe it. You can also find cheap transcription services online. Most smartphones have a voice recording function, and it can be fun to "think out loud" into your recorder, then build content from your own unique voice.

- Use easy templates to focus your writing. You can buy ready-made newsletter templates online, either with or without content. Customize them to your own liking. They give you a great starting point. Don't be afraid to modify to suit your own needs. It's just like house renovations: when you a buy a home you are looking at the bones, then add your own taste in the kitchen counters or new carpet.

- Or use bullet points—it's easier to write articles in bullet points rather than as great slab of text (for one, you don't need to tinker with transitions). It's less daunting and easier to organize your thoughts. Bullet points are also easier to read. Your customers are busy and they're more apt to scan your article while multitasking than sit back with a cup of coffee to peruse a thousand words. Remember, you want to complement their life, not dominate it.

- Numbered lists work like bullet points, and also help the listed items feel connected to each other. "22 Ways to..." or "11 Don'ts For..." are fun to write, and move quickly. Again, don't get hung up on perfection—if you've only got 9, just re-title your Top Ten!

- Not sure what you have to say about your subject? Try the Q&A method in the template I've included at www.AlwaysConnectBook.com.

- Collect links: Make part of your newsletter a section devoted to useful links you've curated from around the web. Add links you think might be interesting to your readers, with a brief introduction. Consider giving this section a cute, catchy name and compiling these links into an easy-to-find box within the newsletter.

- Incorporate sidebars or boxes. An article doesn't have to be just linear text. If some parts of the article—whether it's a quote or a statistic—are truly dynamic and thought-provoking, maybe they need to stand apart from the crowd. This breaks up the copy and highlights the article's important points, and gives you opportunities for the layout.

- Keep it simple. One article, one subject. It's easier to write when you're addressing a single point. This will also help you focus the message so that it's clear and understandable to the reader.

- Get to the point quickly. News reporters use what's called the "inverted pyramid" to tell the story. In other words, the most important and most interesting stuff is on the top, with everything else thereafter in order of importance. If a reader doesn't have time to finish the article, he or she will have at least captured the crucial information. It's also a tool to guide editors in reducing word-count, if needed. What's at the top would never, ever be cut while the ancillary details at the bottom of the story are lower-stakes.

- Cut out unnecessary words. Take another tip from news writing: words have to earn their keep. Use the right word in the best place possible and delete words that aren't pulling their weight. You'll make your writing snappier, easier to read and more engaging. It's nearly impossible to do this on your first draft. Think of this as a task for your second, maybe even third, draft. Try to avoid passive language.

- Invite the reader in, verbally and visually. Headlines are among the most important elements of your newsletters. They act as salesmen for your articles. Writing a good headline increases the chances of your article being read. Make sure your headline gives people a reason to read the article. If your article is there to help the reader, telegraph how it helps. If you're writing about something unusual or fascinating, put that tidbit of information up there in the headline. Look for ways to make your content fresh—for example, if a story is about a dry topic like estate planning, use a word like "surprising" in the headline to cue the reader this isn't going to be like every other boring article on the topic. Maybe "The Surprising Way to Avoid Estate Planning Mistakes" or "3 Things You Probably Don't Know about Estate Planning."

- As well as the boxes and sidebars we discussed above, break your text up with subheads. A page crammed with text is intimidating. The reader might think in a panic, 'But I don't have an hour to read through this!' Make the job of reading your newsletter appear easy. Break up the copy into more manageable sections, and give each a mini-headline. If you think carefully about each section and create headlines based on the most important information, you'll be able to tell the heart of the article with the subheads alone, giving busy readers an overview of the content in a few seconds. This can be a great self-test before sending out your newsletter: if readers only had time to read the subheads, what would they take away about your business?

INSPIRATION SOURCES

You probably have a lot of ideas for stimulating, fascinating articles in your head right now. But here's the danger. If you don't start keeping an eye out for these gems of ideas, the evasive little devils will disappear on you. As I said before, when inspiration strikes, write it down. Maybe you don't have the item you normally log these ideas in, but you can still write them down somewhere, like a napkin or a piece of scrap paper or the back of an envelope. Here are some places to look for inspiration:

- Take a topic currently in the news and put your own twist on it. Now, you might be wondering: How the heck do I take a political topic and pull that into my marketing plan? Here's how one web-hosting company, A2 Hosting, turned a news item into a compelling offer to customers. It's outdated now, of course, but when it was issued this conveyed the impression of timeliness, immediacy and relevance. This is what the newsletter stated: "The U.S. government has called for an economic stimulus, and we at A2 Hosting have an economic stimulus of our own. Use your government economic stimulus check and tax refund to pay up front for your web hosting and save some dough! By pre-paying for your hosting, your monthly hosting fees will drop significantly..."

- Check out content in local and national newspapers, in magazines, on TV talk shows or in panel discussions at industry meetings. Of course, you want to avoid re-printing the article or duplicating the information provided (if you do, be sure to check out the copyright policy), but if you re-interpret them for your clients by adding local content, and your personality, these articles become valuable sources of inspiration. Be wary of fly-by-night coverage. There's nothing more boring than old news. We don't know when a topic will no longer become relevant, but we can guess that if an issue only recently became "hot," it may soon turn cold. Because your newsletter isn't immediate, don't include anything too newsy. Stick to magazine-type stories on subjects with staying power. Remember to check your sources—don't get caught by a site with sloppy reporting or bad facts, or worse, accidentally reprint satire from *The Onion* as if it's true!

- Read others' newsletters. You have suppliers, and you likely belong to associations, clubs, hobby groups and a whole host of other organizations. Some of these send newsletters. Read—or at least flip through—all of them. If you see a story you want to borrow (this is called a reprint), get permission from the company publishing that newsletter (more on this in the next chapter.) In most cases, they'll be happy with a mention and a thank-you.

- Look at what's trending on social media. How can you use this information in your newsletter? A word of warning: Be judicious. As you well know, you can't believe everything you read on the Internet. And always, always avoid the big three: politics, sex and religion. These topics are controversial and could very well cost you a few customers.

- Your local tourism board or visitor's center likely has a website. Peruse it often. What's promotable about your city and how can you play off it? What are the hot new trends in your business community?

- Anecdotes you run across in the course of daily life, such as really good, side-splitting jokes and other people's back stories about what made them who they are today. People get enough bad news from the media. Make them smile and forget the bad news. They'll be grateful.

- Tap into local experts such as a tax accountant, real estate specialist, insurance and mortgage professionals, school principals, doctors, etc. Ask a trusted expert to write a column for you on subjects that will be useful to your customers.

- Regularly read websites and blogs. Intentionally choose those tied to topics in the field of your expertise, and what your newsletter covers. Note that the same warning applies as with social media: Be sure the sites are legit, and the content isn't questionable. And remember that copyright protection applies to online sources as well—get permission for direct reprints.

GETTING IT DONE: HOW TO CREATE AN ONGOING ARTICLE PLAN

Success comes only to those who keep publishing their newsletter. You won't get much traction if you do it just once or twice. Those are just blips on your customers' radar. You want to be a consistent presence in their mailbox, whether it's an email in-box or the one at the end of the driveway. When you send out a newsletter regularly—over a long period of time—people notice and the business flows. It's just like a relationship, really: a quick hello every six months won't cut it. You have to keep nourishing that relationship so it blossoms into a partnership or a client. Keeping in touch over the long term, through good times and bad times and even when you don't feel like it, is what make a relationship strong.

Make the process easier by coming up with ideas for content or even complete articles well in advance (check back with the inspiration sources list!). That way you won't have the "What will I write this month?" panic. Use a chart, a spreadsheet, or calendar software to plan articles for the next 12 months to make keeping track of writing, editing and layout deadlines much easier. You can find a sample newsletter planner at www.AlwaysConnectBook.com.

THE BORING—BUT ABSOLUTELY ESSENTIAL—STUFF YOU MUST DO

Your newsletter should reflect the personal, professional services or quality products you provide. That doesn't mean it has to read like The Wall Street Journal. But it shouldn't sound like a book of jokes or a satirical newspaper (unless you're a working comedian). For many small businesses, it doesn't really matter if your newsletter looks a little rough around the edges. In fact, it may read as a positive—the charity in our case study at the beginning of this chapter was better off with a simple and heartfelt letter rather than a slick production. Readers will, hopefully, see that you made this yourself, and therefore you care.

If you want to get noticed, don't be so polished.

- Seth Godin, entrepreneur and author

As long as it comes straight from your heart and reflects your commitment to providing customers with great useful info, your newsletter will be successful. And your customers won't mistake it for more corporate blah-blah, which they are likely tired of reading.

What you will want to do, however, is make sure there aren't any spelling mistakes and that your numbers (statistics and facts, such as population numbers or percentages) add up. A newsletter riddled with errors will look amateurish and (even worse) as if you don't care enough (or are too lazy) to make sure it's presentable. A potential client might imagine you to be just as careless when doing a business transaction!

If you have two or three people on your team, or even within your social circle, who have a good eye for detail (the more the merrier), definitely run your newsletter by them before going to press. This is not so much to get feedback on the content—although that can be useful for the future—but for a last-minute check to make sure there aren't any typos. Because this can often be a rush job, as in, 'Do you have time in the next 24 hours to proof my newsletter?' try to give your proofreaders a good idea about when their services will be needed as well in advance as possible. Indicate what week of the month it will be, and touch base while you are working on the newsletter to further hone in on the date your newsletter will be ready for proofing.

You don't want to steal other peoples' material, of course. Instead, you want to develop content tailored to your customers and readers. If someone has written articles just for you or even if you want to confirm that you—as the writer—didn't duplicate someone else's sentences by accident, run your copy through a website like Copyscape (www.copyscape.com). What this site does is identify material that has already appeared elsewhere.

If you want to re-use entire articles from websites, print magazines or newspapers, you must ask for permission before reprinting. Usually there will be a policy published on the website or in the publication explaining how to contact them for permissions. If you don't get an OK from the original publication, you risk a lawsuit. Plus, it's courteous to the original author.

Finally, if you use quotes—which add credibility to your content—ensure that you identify where they originated from, whether it's a person or a published book. It's useful to explain in two or three words who this person or author is (as I did above with the quote from Seth Godin), in case readers are not familiar with the source.

THE TAKEAWAY

Good stories are everywhere. When you start thinking about your newsletter, you'll start to see stories in places you never did before. Your job is to cast these stories in a way that suits your audience.

Don't sit and stare at a blank screen with mayhem in your heart. Just start. Even the worst graphophobe can be cured by just getting something—anything—down on the page. Take the first step!

THE EXERCISE

Let's brainstorm: write down 10 topics that will be useful, engaging and interesting to your customers. Don't think too much, and it's okay if they're general. You can always narrow the focus later. But first you need a starting point!

For example:

- Local education/sports/other activities
- Town history
- Local guides to important addresses, emails and phone numbers such as: doctors, drugstore, schools, community centers
- Customer testimonials
- My day: Describe—maybe even hour by hour—what you (a real estate agent/accountant/ insurance or mortgage professional/ entrepreneur, store owner) do in a typical work day.
- Links to interesting articles in other publications or blogs (short introductions to links are an easy content-generator).
- Job-related tips such as, "It's tax time!" or "How do you prepare and/or hold an open house?" or

"What do you look for when insuring your second home?"

Come up with headlines for each topic—based on the list you created just now—and write them below. Here are some starters:

- (great quote): A Profile of _________
- Do You Know Where ________?
- Seen In and Around Town (events)
- Three Things You Must Know to ________
- Five Tips on ___________ Like a Pro

There are lots of ways to start the process of writing your articles. One of the best is the question-and-answer method. Write down the five most common questions associated with each of your 10 topics and then answer them. As an example, for the story entitled "It's 4 pm. Do You Know Where Your Kids Should be?" you might use these questions:

- Are your kids inside glued to their computers and TV or are they outside playing?
- How can you encourage your kids to abandon their entertainment devices?
- What kinds of activities can you do with your kids outside?
- What are the benefits of play?
- What's available in town for your kids to learn an outdoor sport?

AND…

Now you're starting to think like a newsletter editor. Congratulations!

What I want to add at this juncture is this simple statement: making newsletters is fun. Otherwise, I wouldn't have spent the last nine years of my life—and a lot of thinking, planning and writing—helping people make newsletters.

Being a small-business owner isn't easy. You need to take time for some fun. And once you start to receive enthusiastic comments back about your newsletter, you'll realize just how much fun you're having. Have you gotten good feedback on an article idea? Let me know at **www.AlwaysConnectBook.com**

Overcoming Production Phobia

CHAPTER 8

If you think graphophobia is bad, a lot of people find production phobia to be even worse. In fact, it can be crippling and cause many to back out of opportunities that might otherwise boost their income. And we definitely don't want to walk away from those, right? But I'm here to help.

In this chapter, I'll explain how to make the production function easier. If that doesn't work for you, and you've still got rattled nerves, I'll show you how to find and negotiate with the professionals. These folks can do it for you, leaving you to focus on what you do best, which is running your business. Heck, I'll even give you a template for commissioning writers so that you can get through that process with ease.

If you're organized, the process of publishing your newsletter can go swimmingly…most of the time. As with any project there will be some snags and delays. Be sure to build in a cushion of empty time to accommodate these. In other words, don't start proofing the day before your newsletter is due to the printer, and don't start writing the articles three days before you plan to send it out. Believe me, you will experience snags—but don't see these as obstacles or hurdles. Instead, they are experiences in which you learn how to do things better the next time. That said, you can definitely reduce the odds of last-minute crises by planning ahead and developing a production schedule that works for you. It doesn't have to be a complete road map, just a rough guide. It might go something like this…

YOUR MONTHLY NEWSLETTER SCHEDULE

Monday of Week 1:

Develop a list of possible article topics. Consider leaving your desk and doing this activity in a different environment—such as a local coffee shop or even a conference room in your office—as a change of scenery sometimes unlocks your creativity. Either start writing those articles or commission writers immediately.

Monday of Week 2:

Receive articles back from writers, edit for style and accuracy, and place in layout. Use your own simple design, or one of many templates available online.

Monday of Week 3:

Proofread! Use your own fresh eyes after a no-newsletter weekend, or get a trusted friend or super-accurate colleague to spot grammatical errors, typos, incorrect captions on photos, numbers that don't add up, and anything else unpleasing to the eye. Hint: one professional proofreading technique is to read a sentence backwards—you're likely to find errors you might not otherwise catch. Try it!

Monday of Week 4:

Send an electronic file of your newsletter to the printer or to your e-mail subscribers.

If you use this template and the article-writing templates in the previous chapter, I guarantee you it won't be that onerous. It may seem scary now to take on a massive publishing project—every month!—but once you get the hang of it, regular publishing will be a breeze. The key is to develop an organized system. In time you'll view flowing the copy into the template as a piece of cake, and ideas for articles will come to you all month long. You can even view this venture as taking a short break from all the weighty business items that tend to take over your life.

If, however, you're starting to tremble at the idea of laying out your newsletter, or the idea of adding one more thing to your bursting to-do list breaks you out in hives, strongly consider hiring the pros. Even with those great templates you're probably going to fall into a production phobia. And that could wreck other areas of your business life if you don't seek help.

HOW TO HIRE HELP

Some people get pleasure out of publishing a newsletter while others find it as excruciating as a dentist visit. Knowing which camp you lie in is key, and the faster you can figure this out the sooner you can start reaping the rewards of your newsletter.

Assess the hours it's going to take to publish a quality newsletter, one that publishes on a steady and consistent basis and truly reflects your business's personality. If it sounds horribly stressful instead of fun, it's better to face the music now. Don't allow yourself to get overwhelmed! Ask yourself: is this, honestly, something you can do well? Do you have the skills in place? Are you excited? If this doesn't sound like you, try turning the job over to professionals. There are writers, designers, production coordinators, proofreaders, printers and even mailing houses eager to earn a spot on your publishing team. You can pass out just the jobs you least enjoy, or delegate the entire process from getting ideas to hitting send.

If you choose to farm out some or all of this process, first write a brief summary you can send to your professional contributors. Outline your expectations (like a job description but much simpler) and a timeline for each newsletter's production cycle. This protects you and everyone involved by setting out specifically what you want done and when. Imagine that it's the day before an article is due and you drop an email to someone who agreed to pen a story, reminding them their final copy is due tomorrow—and you get back an out-of-office reply: they're on vacation for the next 10 days! By starting with a clear brief, you make sure that all people involved at every stage of production understand your intentions for this publication.

Hiring professionals won't take all the pressure off—you still have to provide guidance and quality control—but it does save you time.

You're probably wondering how to find these savvy, skilled professionals. There are several online staffing platforms where you can post your job description. Upwork (www.upwork.com), for example, boasts thousands of freelance writers, editors, website developers and designers worldwide. You'll be able to see work samples and recommendations to help decide on the right people for the job. Freelancer.com and Guru.com are other sources of help. There are listings for editors and ghostwriters on the Editorial Freelancers Association website (www.the-efa.org) and the Editors Association of Canada (www.editors.ca); you can also find content writers on LinkedIn.

- Be open to their location: with the internet, your perfect designer could live two states away and it won't matter at all.
- Cheapest isn't always best. Many online hiring sites have a large proportion of overseas workers, whose lower local standard of living lets them come in with consistently low bids. Some of them are amazing; others are worth what they charge—and it's not a bargain. Check references and examine past project samples.

It's important to have a writer who understands what you want to achieve with this newsletter and can—this is important—write articles that easily meet that aim. If you have to keep reminding your writer to focus on the top reason you are publishing a newsletter in the first place, that is time lost. But do expect a period of time for the writer to ramp up. After three or four issues, he or she should have a good understanding of issues relevant to your business and be able to explain them to a lay audience. You should be happy with the tone and style by then, too.

Keep the lines of communication open. Ask questions if you're not sure about or don't understand something the writer has included in the submitted article. If you're asking this question, chances are your readers will too, so it benefits everyone to further define the answers. By the same token, be prepared to answer prospective and hired writers' questions. The role of a writer in what we call a "work-for-hire" situation is to nail the voice and style of the client. He or she is eager for you to be satisfied—so be very transparent about what you want to see.

In establishing good relationships with your writers it's important to pay promptly. Writers will be more willing to go the extra mile next time you work with them if they aren't still chasing down your check. Both Upwork and Guru allow you to pay by escrow. The money is there, but you don't release it until you are satisfied with the job completed. Arbitration systems help solve disputes, in case that's ever needed.

When commissioning writers (and your other professional newsletter contributors), you get best results by being very clear about what you need. The following template provides information to help writers as they bid on your projects. It also helps you evaluate these bids as they come in, and ultimately ensures that you get the kind of article you dreamed about. Design it to suit your needs. Here's what a bid invitation or project assignment could look like:

Project name: (e.g., articles about health for newsletter)

Number of articles required: (e.g., four articles, 300 words each)

Copyright: (e.g., I will buy copyright of all articles)

Deadline: (e.g., one week after project is awarded)

Writer requirements: (e.g., You must have already written about health, exercise and nutrition topics for a general audience, and be knowledgeable in these topics. Please show examples of prior work. You must be able to write in a lively, accessible style.)

Reader profile: (e.g., the typical reader is a college-educated mother of two interested in optimizing her children's health. She is busy, doesn't have much time to read books or even long articles on the web or in magazines, but will definitely invest time and money in information and products that help her reach her—and her family's—health goals.)

Article style: (e.g., because our readers are busy, articles should be easy to read—use sub-heads, bullet points, etc, to guide them through. Make the information dense and punchy—no fluff. Accuracy is essential.)

Article topics: (e.g., one to five tips to encourage children to eat vegetables; simple exercises you can do at home without visiting the gym; 10 foods packed with vitamins children need; quick and easy breakfasts for busy parents.)

Other notes: (e.g., Communication is very important to me, so please don't hesitate to contact me if you have any questions or need clarification while writing your article. Please make sure this is all your original work—articles will be checked against Copyscape. This will be a regular gig for the right person.)

Note that you need to always be able to think ahead so that writers have time to do their jobs. You can't come up with an idea for an article—maybe while on the treadmill at the gym you think, 'Yeah! That would be the perfect article for my newsletter!'—and expect the writer to complete it in two business days. Once you've found a good writer or writers, consider assigning several stories at one time, so that you'll be, say, two or three months ahead. Just like anyone, the writers you hire have busy professional and personal lives. Build their trust by learning to respect that.

OTHER PROFESSIONALS

You also will need a competent designer experienced with newsletters. Don't make the mistake of thinking that your cousin's friend who lays out pages for the local glossy magazine is automatically a good fit; the skills needed differ across the spectrum. Make sure candidates understand exactly what you need and don't have "designer's disease." This is defined (by me) as concentrating solely on design (like pretty lines, photoshopped pictures and complicated graphics) without focusing on what you want to ultimately achieve with that design. You need someone who "gets" what you're trying to do, someone who is completely on board with your message—or at least knows how to help you translate it.

It's also important that you have a good relationship with the people employed at your printer, as this will save you problems down the line. Always be nice, polite and interesting, so you quickly become a favorite customer. Not all printers are easy to work with, so make sure you evaluate them on customer service as well as on product and price. Get several quotes, and make sure each printer understands the number of copies of your newsletter you will need, the type of paper you want it printed on, and how you will deliver files to them. For example, will you bring in a flash drive or will you upload to Dropbox or elsewhere on the cloud, or maybe even the printer's own website?

Finally, unless you are prepared to do it yourself, you'll need a production coordinator. This task can easily evolve into the labor equivalent of a part-time job. It's important you have someone who can coordinate work between your writer, designer and printer. A good editor may be able to do this, but be aware that many printers require a high level of technical expertise from their clients. All editors know how to slice and dice sentences and pen eloquent prose, but few editors are sufficiently comfortable with the tech components of your newsletter to interface with your printer.

Proofreaders are worth their weight in gold. However casual your newsletter is, it shouldn't include typos and it should definitely have a consistent style. Proofreaders will catch those typos. You need to establish a certain consistent style and be sure everyone knows what it is and is committed to maintaining it. Consider setting up a "style sheet" with commonly used names and industry jargon defined and correctly spelled and capitalized. It shouldn't take more than an hour for that person to proof your newsletter (or your newsletter's probably too long). Pay handsomely—a flat or per-word fee is best—because some potential clients will be turned off by a typo or sloppy grammar.

PHOTOS: IF IT'S ON THE INTERNET IT'S FREE, RIGHT?

Wrong. It's really not a good idea to copy pictures from the Internet to use in your newsletter. While it might seem like a simple thing to do, think twice before you do it. In a world of social media where images and videos quickly go viral, and they are downloaded thousands of times, it is easy to assume that every single thing published on the web belongs to anyone. This is actually not true. If you want to include them in your newsletter, you'll need a license of some type to do so. Money may not always be involved if you ask first, but the legal fees for making an error will be steep.

It's also just not cool to use other people's work in your newsletter without asking and/or attributing. There are some photographers who are happy to share their images with you, under certain conditions. One way to find these content creators is through Creative Commons, a system set up to give writers and artists a standardized way to grant copyright permissions. Many photographers are happy for you to use their content so long as you give proper attribution.

The way it works is that content creators—such as photographers and graphic designers—add Creative Commons copyright licenses to their gorgeous shots and illustrations. The type of license they choose depends on how they wish the content to be used. Some will allow it to be used in any way under the sun, as long as there is proper attribution. Others don't want their work to be used for any commercial products at all. Find work you like by entering "Creative Commons" + "the subject you're seeking" into the image page of your search engine. When something catches your eye and seems like a good fit with your newsletter, check the type of copyright license it carries. You also may want to consider putting a Creative Commons copyright license on any articles you post online—this will help gain traffic from anyone who chooses to use your content.

You can also purchase stock photos and images. Do the same search, replacing "Creative Commons" with "stock photo" and you'll come up with a host of images you can pay a (usually reasonable) fee to use.

THE TAKEAWAY

Whether you decide to handle all, some, or none of the production process, hopefully you now see how important a role you—or a team of crack professionals—can play in the success of your newsletter. Remember that planning is key to a happy and smooth publication process.

THE EXERCISE

It's now time for an easy, but important, exercise. Develop a monthly schedule of newsletter tasks, similar to the one I discussed at the beginning of this chapter. Be realistic and make sure you are allowing lots of extra time near your publication date. Work ahead by a week if you have to—this will decrease the likelihood you'll experience stress when it comes time to proofread, make final edits and send your newsletter to the printer (or, if it's an email newsletter, hit the "send" button). Consider this a flexible document. After you've gotten a few newsletters under your belt you'll be able to refine the process, perhaps adding an extra week to your schedule, spreading a task over two weeks or merging tasks into one.

AND:

In the next chapter we'll look at the finer points of mailing lists, how to sign people up through your website, permission marketing and more of the nuts and bolts about building your tribe of readers. Meanwhile, if you want to bounce some of your planning concerns off me, reach me at **www.AlwaysConnectBook.com**.

Building The Perfect Mailing List

CHAPTER 9

In the beginning, there were your customers—and they were great customers, YRCs, the best you could ever ask for. Soon they multiplied. And yet more of YNCs were needed to allow the business to grow, both in scope and in profits. Thus began the quest for subscribers impressed with your content (and your business) and who vote with their feet or thumbs or mouse-clicks: buying what you have to sell.

The rest, as they say, is history.

Or is it? Are you really done with the next venture within your business once you start sending out newsletters? Truthfully, you've just hit the tip of the iceberg and there is a lot more coming at you. By walking you through the next phase, my hope is that you will be prepared, and greet this period with enthusiasm, instead of bewilderment.

In using newsletters as the perfect way to retain a loyal customer base and attract new supporters, you face several key decisions. Do you turn to e-mail, print or a combination of the two as your publishing medium? What will be your ROI? How will you maximize the benefits of the new technology? How will you build a clean mailing list?

This whole process can be complex. But fear not: This chapter, and the next two, provides you with everything you need to know about distributing your newsletter in a way that is best for you and your business. Not every newsletter publisher follows the same rules or the same methods—but I can help you make a wise choice.

Let's start with building a list of subscribers.

UNDER CONSTRUCTION

A clean lead and client database is among the greatest assets of any business. Maintaining, adding to, and nurturing your client list is probably one of your most important jobs as a business owner. Once your distribution list is established, it offers all kinds of tag-along opportunities for sending other forms of marketing communications, such as notices of flash sales, exclusive subscriber offerings and surveys. Take the time you need to build this list and the pay-off is huge. Do you want to announce a weekend sale via an email blast on a Thursday? Great! All you have to do is click a few buttons and the word is out. But if you had to start researching email addresses (as well as physical addresses) for all of your clients and plug them into a database, that could literally take weeks. You've now missed your window of opportunity.

Want to know the bonus of building the "perfect" distribution list? It works whether you plan to send your communications by email or by mailing printed copies. (Or both—which is my preference. More on this later.)

I've often said that a well-maintained mailing list is key to your business's success…or its failure. You're probably wondering how it can be both. After years in this business, it's very easy for me to tell whether an entrepreneur will be successful or not. I'm not trying to be judgmental or critical. It simply comes down to one factor: How quickly is he or she growing those contact lists?

Whenever I have clients who are disappointed with the results of their emailed newsletter, they show a very typical pattern. It goes something like this. They join Ready To Go Newsletters enthusiastically and upload their contact list. Usually that list is between 100 and 200 people. They then send their newsletters to that list for perhaps four to six months. If it's a monthly newsletter that is four to six issues.

And that's it. That list never grows. Indeed, what happens is that over time, the number of people on the list slowly declines as people change email addresses or decide to unsubscribe. Their list withers. What is the person publishing this newsletter doing wrong? Why are people unsubscribing or not making the choice to deepen their business relationship?

It's not enough just to load your initial list into the system and then hope that will fuel you for the future. It won't. By the end of year one, many of these people will have changed email addresses, switched careers or unsubscribed. In fact, this will happen every year without you doing anything. It's just how things work.

So, here's the secret to growing your business and stopping it from declining: you absolutely need to increase the number of people you are in touch with. Even in the world of printed newsletters, it's rare to have more than 75% of your subscribers read your words—fewer than that if you are sending emails. The more people that subscribe, the more leads you have. Failure to grow your list of contacts could mean your business doesn't just stay static, it slides backwards.

Where else can you acquire names and addresses for your list? From your new client intake form, or an in-store opportunity near the cash register where people provide their contact information on a small card. Make sure you get their permission for any electronic mailings—we will talk more about that in a later chapter. Remember that one contact who signs up on purpose is worth more than a hundred spam emails to people who don't know who you are.

Successful list-builders put forms on their websites to collect new names. On my Ready to Go Newsletters website, there's a form right there on the home page. People can add their information while I'm sleeping or on a plane—I don't need to do it for them. Plus, if our interaction is rushed, all I have to do is provide my website address and they do the rest. These clients make good use of the bonus reports I provide, used as a "magnet" to encourage people to join their list. (They'll say something like: 'Join my list and get this valuable information for free.')

Successful list-builders remember their number-one-job is to collect high-quality leads. Every time they meet someone in a business context, they ask if they can add his or her name to the list. Every single marketing piece they produce mentions the bonus report (or the right "magnet" for their business) and encourages people to sign up to receive it.

They send an email newsletter to each prospect and client at least once a month. This is important. Anything less frequent than that is almost pointless because you'll be a mere drop in the ocean. Indeed, many people contact their database much more often than monthly.

Here's the thing. A business is a living organism. You need to feed it. If you don't, it just withers away and dies. Yes, it requires work. But it's better than the alternative, which is closing up shop.

FINDING SUBSCRIBERS

Here are a few suggestions that can help you start to build a great mailing list:

- Put an offer on the back of your business cards to get people to sign up. Consider a colored background so it stands out in a stack spilled on one's desk after a networking event.
- At tradeshows, bring a sign-up book. Ask those who sign up or give you their business cards if you can send them emails. Be sure to ask for permission.
- Host a seminar and ask those who attend to sign up for additional information on the seminar topic. Consider even sending them a special email—with information related to the seminar's topic—before they receive their first newsletter issue.
- Create a birthday club where you give people a "gift" for signing up. They'll feel great when you remember their birthday each year—and there are newsletter apps that do that for you.
- Empower your employees to add customers and prospects to your mailing list, and reward them for doing so.
- Offer a discount or coupons to customers or leads in exchange for their contact information.
- Ensure you follow up on emails that bounce. Each time this happens, try to get the correct email address. Call for an updated email address, and use

the opportunity to re-build your relationship with the customer.

- Make space in your newsletters for a link to a complementary business's subscriber form. Ask that business to do the same for you. (if you're in real estate, perhaps your favorite mortgage broker.)

- Put subscriber forms on every page of your website in a prominent position. Some might find your website through a google search that takes them to a certain page—make sure it's always one with a subscriber form.

- Include a forward-to-a-friend link in your newsletters. The link should connect to the page containing the information deemed of value to the friend, and should include a sign-up form. Meet potential subscribers more than half-way: make sure the process is easy and can be done in two or three clicks.

- Include a newsletter sign-up link in the signature of all your personal emails.

- Require people to provide their emails to access special information or offers that are available to be downloaded. Don't let them walk away without capturing a way to contact them later!

- Offer newsletter recipients privileged access to bonus reports and other valuable information. Think of your newsletter list as an insider's club. Include the value they'll receive, such as "specialized tips" or "insider's secrets."

For a more subtle gathering technique, work the blogs and forums that your prospects likely read. Offer insightful comments to articles or blog posts, and include a link to your subscribers' form in your signature. Ask if you can write a guest post.

Do make promises you can keep. One-well established author offered her subscribers a series of promises that she was careful to follow through on. She promised "not to bombard their inboxes," to always deliver quality content, and to offer each subscriber the chance to win free e-books, as well as enjoy access to exclusive content.

Make it easy to register. This may look like I'm stating the obvious, but you'd be surprised at the circumnavigation customers must go through to sign up on some sites. If you were that customer would you keep trying to solve the puzzle or go on with your day? I think you know the answer! Try for two clicks—one to get to your page, one to hit enter and send your information. More than three clicks will lose you a fair number of subscribers in our short-attention-span world.

Consider who receives your email. Are you sending emails to just one list—with all sorts of prospects—or are you segmenting your list according to your subscribers' interests? You don't have to limit yourself to one email list. A life coach might offer a client newsletter to her clients in addition to a weekly newsletter to all of her contacts, with the hope that some might read her words and think, 'Yeah, I'd like to hire her!'

When you hit the "send" button on your emails without thinking about the needs of each subscriber, you risk alienating him or her. Someone might read the introductory newsletter, think it's written for novices, and promptly unsubscribe. Or, a beginner to the topic you advocate in an insiders-tips letter might feel intimidated and decide to leave the list. Even worse, you're missing out on opportunities to attract new customers when your loyal subscribers re-tweet your information or "like" you on social-media sites. Segment your customer list. One newsletter is not going to work for your entire customer base. How do you segment? I'm glad you asked...

ALL ABOUT SEGMENTATION

Segmentation may sound difficult and time-consuming, and mildly stressful, but it's really not once you get your head around it. Basically, you'll customize your subscribers into categories. You're going to take that broad market of "everyone who has ever wanted to buy anything" and divide it into subsets of people with common needs and priorities. That way, you can design your own strategy to reach them, enlighten them, and eventually, make them your customers.

Start by profiling your current customers and coming up with commonalities between them. Depending on your product or service, you can group customers by geographical location, lifestyle, attitudes, behaviors...or any number of other factors. Make sure the variables are relevant to your business. Maybe, with a roofing business, whether or not customers have children is not important but a car dealer will really want to know household demographics because some shoppers want a sports car while others need a mini-van.

If, for example, you market products and services to other businesses (this is called B2B, or business-to-business) you could divide up the market according to the following. How do they use your product? What is the size and frequency of their orders or the length of time they've been customers? (The answers to those last two questions could indicate their loyalty to you as a supplier.)

If you market products or services to consumers (B2C, or business-to-consumer), you have a wide range of variables, such as: education, age, gender, income, attitudes, and lifestyles. Or you could look at buying behavior: How do people use your product? How loyal are they to your products versus your competitors' products? How sensitive are they to price? You might even want to dig deeper. Do people tend to spring for your products only when they are on sale? Or are they only buying your cheaper products? The answer to retaining their business could be as simple as breaking down your services into smaller quantities.

You can make it even easier by segmenting your customers according to what they currently buy or have bought from you in the past. When preparing your newsletter, include information on new products and services that might interest them, similar to the products they have purchased or are purchasing now.

By understanding each group (segment) as much as you can, you can create messages that are more relevant. Not only does this save you time, but because you're honing in on their particular interests you're making them feel special—and customers who feel valued will not leave you. Looking back to earlier chapters on building loyal relationships with YRCs, this is yet another great way to retain their business—offer information and discounts on the products and services they really need and want.

Another benefit of segmentation: you can identify opportunities to launch new products or services. Or you may find ways to polish up what you currently offer. Maybe that one-on-one consultation can work for both seasoned customers and those new to your tribe. It's all how you frame it. Seasoned customers may appreciate the consultation as a "check-in" or "fine tuning" while the newbies will love viewing it as an "assessment of your household needs." By repackaging, you'll soon find it easier to focus on your most profitable customers. The result is a better return on investment (ROI).

A word of warning: Don't bite off more than you can chew. I've found that it's best to create only three or four segments. Otherwise you are going to have a lot of overlap, not to mention many balls in the air at once. Say you have five segments. Are you prepared to send out emails five-fold each month? Although initially there may be a limited number of customers in each segment (hopefully, these will grow as you continue to add new names and emails to your list) the point is that it's manageable. There's no doubt you'll have the time and money to serve these customers well.

Here's a great example inspired by an article in Investopedia on a manufacturer of athletic shoes. Lots of different kinds of customers buy different kinds of shoes for different sports. This means the consumer playing field for athletic shoes is broad. A marathoner, for example, would be unlikely to buy or know more about shoes worn by basketball players, and vice versa. The great opportunity is two newsletters: one with news on the IRONMAN Triathalon and a coupon for sports gel; another with a profile on the NCAA championship coach.

Or say you're a real estate agent. One easy way to segment customers is by demographics. You might find they break down nicely into young families, first-time buyers and empty-nesters (retirees or those about to be retirees). You can approach these segments in different ways:

The empty-nesters will likely be interested in articles on downsizing, the pros and cons of moving across the country to be with kids and grandkids, staging, condo living, five tips on selecting a good mover, selling antiques, etc. You could even focus on cultural events or city life—what's happening near the condo they'd like to buy?

Young families will be interested in tips on selling their starter homes and moving up to larger-sized homes, decluttering and organization, even charities that accept used toys.

New buyers will like tips on qualifying for a mortgage or finding the right neighborhood, and stories on remodeling projects and the value they add (or don't add) to their properties—this could be anything from an actual remodel in the neighbourhood to how to budget for a dream kitchen.

WHAT NOT TO DO TO SUBSCRIBERS

You'd market differently to a working mom of three kids than you would to a single man without kids, wouldn't you? Marketing Profs guru Elaine Fogel encounters lots of companies who don't follow this basic rule. "How often do you receive emails (or printed materials) with content that has no relevance?" she asks.

For example, take the non-profit organization that failed to check the list of attendees at a recent fundraiser. The organization sent out an email thanking someone for attending. One problem: she didn't actually go. This leaves a bad impression—if the organization can't even adopt a system to record who attends an event, why would someone want to gift them with money or time? And then there's the airline that e-mails special offers for flights...but these flights didn't depart from the subscriber's city. Essentially, this is information that cannot be used or acted upon, and it's a waste of time for the subscriber.

These, Fogel suggests, are classic examples of what not to do to your subscribers. Even if they gush over your business (including your products or services), most won't think twice about hitting the unsubscribe button (or tossing your newsletter into the recycle bin) if your communications are this irrelevant. Their next move could be to move on…to your competitors.

There are also some serious privacy issues that you must respect. As you start to build your list, consider these caveats:

When customers share their personal information, they expect you to safeguard and use it responsibly. They trust you won't lose it, abuse it, sell it to third parties or expose it to cyber-attackers. They assume you'll follow laws regarding privacy and information practices. If you do any of the above, expect to not only lose their business and trust, but also any referrals they may have provided. Worse, they may share with friends and family that you don't care about personal connections at all and that doing business with you is a hollow, empty process. Do you really want to be known as that type of person?

Before you start building a customer database, develop a privacy policy that details the data you're gathering, how it will be used, whether you intend to share this information, and, if so, with whom. If you plan to sell your data to third parties, make this clear in your policy.

Don't ask for too much at once. You don't want people to feel stressed out about providing their contact information. Start with the basics: Name, as well as mail and email addresses. Gradually add other data points, such as age and demographic factors, once you get to know your client. As your relationship deepens with your customers, you can ask them about values, lifestyle, family and personal preferences—all things that will help you help them.

THE TAKEAWAY

Building a good distribution list, constantly adding to it, and ensuring you publish relevant content for your customers, in addition to communicating with them regularly, are all vital to the survival of your company. These tasks must be done regularly and methodically

Of course, you can outsource many of these tasks—and we'll discuss how and to whom in the next two chapters—but you still need to oversee the process as a traffic manager. It may be the difference between success and failure.

THE EXERCISE

Get acquainted—really acquainted—with your mailing list. Sit down with your current mailing list. and think about how you can make it more valuable. Next, consider how you can segment the list. Match up some of the story ideas from chapters 6 and 7 with each segment. Don't worry about making every article 100% relevant to all of your segments. That gets confusing! Just ensure there's at least one article that directly addresses each group.

AND...

In case it isn't already obvious, I believe very strongly that your mailing list is vital to your success. If you have any stories about great (or lousy) lists, send them to me. I'll use some on my website or in my blog as examples for others (with your permission, of course!).
www.AlwaysConnectBook.com

All About Email —For Non-Techies

CHAPTER 10

Let me confess my personal bias up front. Email and print distribution both work well, and in fact we provide both options to our Ready to Go Newsletters clients. The optimal solution is to use both...because they truly complement each other.

Here's why: email newsletters, when sent to people who give you their permission to receive them, will yield a lot of important information. This might include who clicked where and when and, most importantly, did those clicks result in new sales or appointments? And that's extremely valuable—no question about it. Email newsletters are a great way to make timely offers, call your customers to action, and distribute content easily. This is all done with the ability to measure that they've gotten to where you want them to go. Plus, email is cheap. But electronic newsletters lack a physical connection.

Print offers that physical touch. You can hold a printed product in your hands, pass it along, leave it in strategic places, obtain second and third readers...even read it in the bathroom. (This is a unique quality I call "bathroomable," a wacky term I'll discuss further in the print chapter.)

So, here's my bias: I really like the way the two methods complement each other because they give you the maximum bang for your buck. Why choose just one? Send both.

IN PRAISE OF E-MAIL

Email rocks, according to a recent study reported in Marketing Profs. ExactTarget asked some 1,500 U.S. consumers which marketing channel they prefer to receive the promotional emails they subscribe to. More than three-quarters answered that email was their preference. Turns out, its online competitors weren't even close: only 4% of the survey respondents picked Facebook, and a dismal 1% selected Twitter.

I recently read a very compelling piece by Navneet Alang in The Globe & Mail on the history of email. Now, you are probably thinking that the history lesson on email would be very short, but hear me out. Alang's conclusion supports the study results above: Email is enjoying an unprecedented revival. Turns out it's the number-one way to reach people today, despite the advent of other online tools like Facebook and Twitter.

Why? As Alang goes on to explain, in those heady days before social media, "this kind of personalized delivery was an exciting prospect, quite different from the top-down distribution of information we were then used to." However, "with the arrival of blogs, then aggregators, then social media—not to mention mountains of e-mail—getting one more tidbit in your inbox started to seem pointless, especially when you could get more than you ever needed simply by checking just a few sites."

In part, it was the loss of Google Reader—where you could read information from many sites compiled in one place—that created a void. Many turned to newsletters, "replacing mass delivery with a more focused one," and newsletters became one way of following ideas and people all in one place. It became the new version of Google Reader, but without "the sometimes-vibrant-sometimes-deafening ebb and flow of Twitter or Facebook."

Alang goes on to explain why. "There's a kind of intimacy between writer and reader, what feels like a one-to-one connection between an author and your inbox...The newsletter is focused, quiet—somehow more like print, or at least a kind of midpoint between it and digital."

While Facebook, Twitter, Instagram, Pinterest and every Next Big Thing are still jockeying for attention, maintaining a huge "social media presence" can drain your time, attention and resources. By subscribing to your email newsletter, readers are saying, "I'm willing to listen—give it a shot." You're able to focus your efforts on serving your unique market segments, rather than having to learn a new strategy for each platform.

HOW NOT TO DO IT

Thanks to better spam filters than were available a few years ago, email distribution is increasingly low-noise. Important emails are not mistakenly going in the "junk" or "spam" folders as they once were. Email delivers your newsletter right to the recipient, and he or she can read it at leisure. By communicating with recipients on their computer or mobile device, your e-mailed newsletter becomes a powerful way to build a relationship.

However, if you abuse the easy access and immediacy of email, you run the risk of losing trust in the marketplace. Here's a tongue-in-cheek look at the many ways to do it all wrong, with a nod to Toby Young's very funny book, How to Lose Friends and Alienate People.

- Attach your newsletter as a 10MB file, justifying it as "It's got beautiful graphics and that's why it's so large. People love spending precious minutes of their lives opening huge attachments! And with so many people checking email on their phones these days, who doesn't want to burn their bandwidth with a big download?"

- Send your newsletter to people who didn't opt-in. Maybe you bought a list of names off some website, or use your-relative-who-forgets-to-BCC's personal email list. All the people who got Aunt Hilda's out-of-date virus warning are going to love you!

- Send your newsletter out every six months, so people don't remember who you are.

- Don't include unsubscribe links in your newsletter. Sure, the law requires you to give recipients at least one unsubscribe link in every email correspondence sent, but you can't make an omelet without breaking a few eggs. Nor can you cause maximum annoyance to potential customers if you don't let them opt-out until after the first fifty emails!

- If a reader does finally figure out how to unsubscribe, make them log in to your website to do it. Of course they have to select a user name they probably can't remember, plus a password containing a capital letter, a number, a symbol, and the tears of a leprechaun.

- Why waste time writing meaningful content that entertains or provides useful information? Fill that space with promotions and lists of how wonderful your business is!

- Be persistent! Incredibly persistent! If anyone unsubscribes or tells you to stop contacting them altogether, just keep on sending the newsletter. You can change their mind, right?

- Why target only the people likely to buy your product or service? Send your newsletter to everyone you can possibly find on this planet without first screening for age, location, income, or level of interest! Maybe that 75-year-old retiree in Boca Raton wants a new snowsuit with hot pink sparkles—she just doesn't know it yet.

- Always send your newsletter whether you have anything to say or not. Any old content will do—it doesn't matter what you send as long as you send something, right?

No, people. Just no. Any of the above is a one-way ticket to Spamville, with your emails getting deleted, maybe even getting a desist order from your email server, and worst of all, alienating potential customers and losing ones you already have.

IS EMAIL DISTRIBUTION FOR YOU?

Most people believe that delivering email is pretty straightforward. You upload a mailing list, create an email, hit "send," and then mighty wizards transport that email to your recipients. Those wizards might even use ancient, handcrafted cables and powerful laser beams.

What more could you possibly need to know about this process?

A lot. Let's start with your Return on Investment and how to quantify the value of an email subscriber.

ROI—EMAILS

A 2013 study by Marketing Sherpa indicates that 92% of respondents believe that email is now (60%) or will eventually (32%) produce a positive return on investment (ROI). (Great news, right?) And when it came to budgeting, 64% believed senior management would increase their budget for email campaigns, compared to 51% who thought their budget for online display advertising would grow. A scant 7% believed they'd get more money for TV and radio ads.

Because email marketing is so inexpensive, the value you get back from it can be very high. Bryan Wade, senior vice-president of email, mobile and content for ExactTarget, was quoted in a recent article in The Guardian: "As far as the return on investment (ROI) that our customers get through email, for every dollar they spend on email marketing they get $40 back. It works. No other digital channel gives you that ROI."

Revenue per subscriber (RPS) is one method of determining ROI. Here's how it works: To calculate the RPS for the year, add all the sales revenue from your email marketing and divide it by the number of email addresses on your (clean) mailing list. (Naturally, that doesn't include the bounce backs. Be sure to remove those from consideration when calculating RPS.)

Of course, this supposedly easy method doesn't work if you aren't able to separate the revenue earned from your newsletters from revenue produced through other marketing channels. If this is the case for you, know that the average cost per action (AC/A) tracks actions taken by responders. It gives each action a monetary value based on the cost of promoting a product to your mailing list versus other methods (like using social media). With other media (those with published rates) you would pay on a cost-per-action basis, so it turns out you already have the value of those media.

If your objective is, for example, to encourage sign-ups for a seminar or specific event, once you know the final number of registrants, you can figure out how much it would have cost per action through Twitter or Facebook, compared to the cost of sending notices to your segmented newsletter email list.

GETTING THAT RESPONSE

There are a number of factors that determine whether an email, especially a bulk email, gets a response from its recipients. Because who wants to write an email—especially a labor-intensive email newsletter—and have it ignored? It's important you know what these factors are.

- Your list: Have people signed up to receive your information, or are you spamming them? Sending unsolicited emails will endanger you in so many ways, as you'll see spelled out in the section on Permission Marketing.

- Subject line: This is a very basic first step but extremely powerful. A great subject line will entice your recipient into opening your email. Here are some things to consider. Is the subject line really relevant to your reader? Does it indicate that the information inside will help him do his job better or make her life better? Will he consider it a must-read? Or is the subject line intriguing enough that she'll open the email out of curiosity? (Once you've built up a good relationship with your list, your recipients will open your newsletter because it comes from you, not because of the subject line. They have learned that your content is valuable to them.)

- Valuable content: How do you know whether your newsletter content is sufficiently valuable? Consider the quality of the information you now publish, such as bonus reports, blog posts and white papers—are they clear, interesting, relevant and engaging? Is your website easy to navigate? Chances are, if the material you are already producing is great, your newsletter will be, too.

- Your reputation: Are you somebody who consistently delivers value? Was the last newsletter you sent worth reading? (Remember, you probably only get one chance with a new subscriber.) Can you be trusted to give independent advice as an expert, not a cheesy salesperson? What is your business's online reputation? Tap into social media to find out what people are saying about you. Your content could be dynamite, but if people hate you and/or your business, they're not going to give you permission to send it to them.

- Pretty versus plain: HTML newsletters are the ones that look pretty. That's because they're designed the same way that web pages are. But it's hard to get HTML right, as different email software will read it differently. If you're not a coding whiz, you can hire experts who focus on coding email newsletter templates. Their expertise enables you to have great design, and integrate your branding, too. But...

- Consider text-only newsletters or newsletters with minimal design. First, they're easier—you don't have to hire experts to create them. Second, they're more personal. After all, when was the last time you sent a fancy email loaded with graphics and illustrations to a friend? Here at Ready to Go Newsletters we send out a lot of plain text emails—we think they make a good connection between us and the people reading them. According to our feedback, they agree.

- Service providers: Choose a really good, highly efficient email-marketing service provider. This company will handle all the complexities, including feedback circuits, bounce messages and connection optimizers.

The bottom line: Response from readers is based on your newsletter's perceived value. Is your email really adding value to your readers' lives? Is it worth the click? Clicks don't come easy. You must work hard for each and every one.

PERMISSION MARKETING

As I said, sending unsolicited emails is pretty much guaranteed to fail. It will be a black strike against your business. What you need is permission marketing. This concept is all about building a trusted relationship with clients and prospects. This means you send information they want to receive. It's about being the go-to guy rather than the pest at the party.

> Permission marketing is the privilege (not the right) of delivering anticipated, personal and relevant messages to people who actually want to get them.
>
> - Seth Godin, social media expert, in his book Permission Marketing

Think about your own email in-box. I bet you have a lot of emails that do not fall into this category. What happens when they arrive? You probably don't even open them, choosing to hit the "delete" button instead.

Seth Godin has written that while a spam campaign can feel like a smart idea, the more you use it, the less your brand is worth. Sending ten thousand emails to a bought list is a limited-window marketing opportunity. Pretty soon, your server will get complaints, your emails will get blacklisted to go right into the spam folder, and you're unlikely to see actual meaningful results. A permission campaign—in which each reader has chosen to receive your material ("subscribe")—only grows in value, until it gets so big that you can build an entire business around it..

Earning permission from subscribers is a long-term, profitable, scalable strategy that pays for itself. Think about how much better off a brand would be if it took extra time to make promises, keep them and be transparent about its communications. Customers probably would not leave, right? You probably have brands and businesses you support just for these very reasons and would never think about using another dry cleaner, child care center, or tax preparer, right?

Of course when you ask someone if it's OK to send them information, it goes without saying that the information has to be valuable in order for them to say yes. They don't want or expect just advertising material. They anticipate interesting content flowing into their email inbox or postal box. And if you don't deliver, well, they need to be able to say "sorry, changed my mind." (Of course, with this book on your side, your content is going to be fantastic, right?)

So whatever way you get permission, make sure there's an easy way to unsubscribe, so that you know you're keeping that permission. And as long as you have that invitation, it's up to you to keep earning it with great, timely, valuable content that speaks to your customers.

EMAIL CONTENT TIPS

Before we get into the nuances of clicks, open rates, hosted versus non-hosted content and new anti-spam legislation in both the U.S. and Canada (not to mention whether to send your newsletters in plain text or HTML), you'll need to arm yourself with some basic information on what, exactly, should be in your newsletter.

- Whose name goes in the from line? Is it your name, or your company's name? I generally recommend the personal touch for real estate agents, accountants, lawyers, and others who provide services, especially those that are high-cost and require a level of trust. Retailers have a choice to go personal or for the team (use company name). But bear in mind the reason you're sending a newsletter is to build a relationship with customers. The only rule is to keep it consistent.

- What's the subject? We talked about this back in the section on how to get a positive response. But this is so important, it's worth saying again: Half of your potential readers decide whether to open your email based on the subject line, according to email service provider VerticalResponse. Make it interesting. Highlight an offer or make it a teaser.

- What does the reader see before they even click? The pre-header is the first line of text (which also appears after the subject line in many email programs, sometimes before even opening the email.) These days, some people are busy enough to set their email preview to show the first three lines—if you don't get their attention, they'll hit delete. Use your pre-header to provide more detail on the subject or set up the value of what's inside. Headlines are another great way to highlight key content and grab "skimmers." Interestingly, 80% of people read headlines but only 20% continue to read the article, so yours should be a grabber.

- Images: Do you want to use pictures to call attention to content and make your email newsletter more readable? If you add an image, don't make it a huge file that takes forever to download or clogs up in-boxes. As VerticalResponse suggests: Use the 80/20 rule—80% text to 20% images.

- Some people turn off their image settings to speed up downloads. You should use alt-text, in conjunction with your images. It will describe the image and how it fits with your content.

- Don't forget to include a call to action. What do you want the recipient to do? Examples are: "Read more..." or "Log in here to see..." or "Get your coupon at this link..."

- Social media: Use links to your website, blog, and Twitter and Facebook accounts. This is a great way to deepen a connection with your customer beyond the newsletter.

DON'T BE SPAM

Did you know that in 2013 almost 70% of the world's emails were classified as spam? According to a 2014 security bulletin from Kaspersky Lab, this rate has dropped slightly (by 2.5%). But the bad news is it's unlikely to continue to go down—the bad guys are always coming up with new ways to scam us. So important is the spam problem worldwide that both the U.S. and Canadian governments have enacted regulations regarding spam.

I'm not an attorney, and my specialty is newsletters, not the spam laws of your jurisdiction. Check the laws that are relevant to you.

In the United States, the CAN-SPAM Act is the main governing law for commercial email. It prohibits false or misleading header information and deceptive subject lines, and also requires you to tell recipients how to opt out of receiving future email. According to CAN-SPAM, you must honor a recipient's opt-out or unsubscribe request within ten business days. The legislation also spells out tough penalties for violators. Even if you hire another company to handle your email marketing, you are still legally responsible.

Meanwhile in Canada, the anti-spam legislation known as CASL took effect on July 1, 2014, when the majority of the Act came into force (other sections became effective in 2015 and some will in 2017). CASL prohibits "sending of commercial electronic messages without the recipient's consent," and "the collection of electronic addresses by the use of computer programs or the use of such addresses, without permission." This collection and use is known as "address harvesting."

This legislative spotlight on spam has made it difficult for small businesses. Many want to send bulk emails through services like Outlook.com or Gmail. I have never recommended this—because most personal email accounts don't make it easy to comply with anti-spam best practices

Why care? Well, we're the good guys, of course. We want to send valuable interesting content to our subscribers, not spam. But just because we're the good guys doesn't mean we're not impacted by the spam issue. With increasingly more sophisticated anti-spam products, there's a strong likelihood that your lovingly produced newsletter may get accidentally caught in a spam filter. There's also the danger that if people report your emails as spam, your email address will get blocked, which of course is terrible news for all your regular communications. But there are ways to have the best chance to get your newsletters delivered, while still protecting your email reputation.

EMAIL SERVICE PROVIDERS

All this sounds hugely complex to master. And it is. But email service providers are here to take care of most of this for you. Bottom line: they help you deliver your newsletters. Popular services include Constant Contact and Mailchimp. I've used AWeber, VerticalResponse and ActiveCampaign, and been pleased with them. It's still important to do your own research to find an email service provider that's right for you. This section may help you hone in on the best fit for your needs

With an email sending service you upload your email list to a website. The service then looks after the design, list management and—finally—sends out the emails. Anyone serious about sending email newsletters needs to use a professional email service, and it's easier to set one up right at the beginning, rather than try to shift your operation over when it gets too big to handle—hopefully soon!

Other benefits of using an email service provider:

- They will add links to each e-mail which give people an easy way to unsubscribe in compliance with legislation (otherwise, you'd have to do the data entry yourself).

- They will also automatically add your physical mailing address to your newsletter (another requirement to comply with anti-spam legislation.)

- An email service provider allows you to add, subtract and move images without fussing with HTML code, or even contacting your webmaster. It ensures your design appears as it is meant to on every size computer monitor or mobile device. If you send out those emails yourself, your design might not translate well on all devices. These days there are many handheld devices to consider—such as tablets, smartphones and laptops—plus desktop computers.

- Email service providers manage your list(s) for you. Because you undoubtedly have multiple and segmented lists, this can become complicated if you opt to do it yourself. On the flipside, it's quite easy to upload your list in a file—or one by one—to a host service. These services also provide web forms you can use to collect emails from your website. The forms are completely automated, freeing you up to run your business.

- They also offer tools for managing contacts, and sign-up boxes to publish on your website so people can join your list. An email service provider can track open rates, bounce rates and unsubscribe stats, as well as determine which links were clicked so you know which offers are working. When people unsubscribe, the service makes sure you don't send your newsletter to them again. (Because this is the quickest and easiest way to lose the trust of a customer or prospect, right?) And if a newsletter has a hard bounce (this is when the recipient's server considers it permanently undeliverable, because of an invalid address or because your server has been blocked), it doesn't get sent again. If someone marks your email as spam, they also are blocked from the list.

- Finally, email services work overtime to ensure your newsletters get delivered. Because they send mail for many clients, they can more easily afford staffers who specialize in 'deliverability'. These days, when so many legitimate emails get blocked, the value of delivery-optimized emails alone is a terrific reason to spend money on an email service.

You've worked hard on your newsletter. You're excited to see where it takes you and how many customers respond. You can't wait to cultivate business with the interest that starts pouring in. Spend the extra cash to be sure your newsletter goes where it should. You won't regret it.

TRACKING AND TESTING

One of the great things about email (and all online marketing) is that you can track and test it. You can determine open rates (how many people opened your email), click rates (how often, and which, links were clicked), unsubscribes and bounces. You can even hone in on the individual recipient's track record in how he or she uses your email: What does this person click on and when? How many times does the person open your email to re-read? Is it being shared on social media? The answers to these questions are invaluable.

Have you ever invited 100 people to a party and only had 20 show up? It would be kind of disappointing, wouldn't it? I'd feel like I was No-Friends-Simon. But, if you actually look at the 20 who did show up, they're your best friends. These are the people you feel closest to, and they're the ones who really matter.

Email newsletters are a lot like that. You send out hundreds, but most people don't take the few seconds to open them. Unfortunately, this is normal. A combination of filled-to-the-brim inboxes, tire-kicker indifference and not-quite-ready-yet inaction depresses open rates. My advice is to not take it personally. You have more than one chance to attract this customer with your email newsletter, after all. People's attitudes towards email differ by the day. On a particularly busy day, it's easy to hit "delete" on anything that's not personal or urgent, while on a slow day, catching up on email is fun!

METRICS DEFINED

Open rate: This is the number of people who have opened your newsletter. Subject lines and the name of the person or company sending the newsletter mostly affect the open rate.

Click rate: This is the number of people who have clicked on a link in your newsletter. Many publishers don't put enough links in their newsletters, which can translate to a low click rate. We recommend you always link back to your website when appropriate, and to any other businesses, publications, authors or websites you cite.

Bounce rate: This is the number of emails that bounced, primarily due to a bad address. People who have not emailed their clients for a long period get a high bounce rate—sometimes over 10%. It's a reason to mail frequently—if you stop mailing, your list starts to die.

Unsubscribe rate: This is the number of people who have unsubscribed from your newsletter. This number should be quite low once your letter is established and you have a solid permission marketing plan in place, but if you're mailing for the first time to people who don't know you well, this number will be higher.

Unfortunately, a lot of small-business people (and big-business folks, too) fixate on open rates—which feel like they signal email success or failure. But to me, the actions that people take after they've opened the email are much more important—like clicking on links, reading articles, getting in touch and buying stuff. Quite simply: Do they contact you and do they hire you? What is the effect on your business over the long term? These are the questions you should be asking. Still, while I don't subscribe to the open-rates-are-all-that-count approach, I do believe it's worth investing time in raising the percentage of subscribers who open your email.

So, along those lines, here are some open rates for the first quarter of 2014 (the most recent available), courtesy of a Yesmail report. The email marketing software provider analyzed 5 billion emails for the time period. It noted that while volume declined after a "mailing-heavy fourth quarter 2013," open rates actually rose by 6%. People were getting less email—but more that they actually wanted.

- For B2B generally, open rates reached an average of 18.7%; for the consumer services industry, it's 12.4%.
- More specifically, the insurance industry boasts the highest average open rate for this time period (31.4%); the financial-services industry came in second with 28%.

A VerticalResponse survey indicates open rates as follows:

- Prospect mailings opens average 11% to 13%
- B2B client mailings opens average around 22%
- B2C client mailings opens average between 15% - 20%
- Non-profit opens average around 15%

Most of my clients are within these ranges. However, your actual open rate will depend on the quality of your list. If it's a list of people who do not know you well, the rate will be lower. If it is a list of people who know you very well, and are already partaking of your services, the rate will undoubtedly be higher.

Don't be discouraged if these numbers seem lower than you were hoping. The figure you should care about most is the impact on your business over the long term. The converse applies as well: Just because you have a high open rate doesn't mean your particular email is going to bring you oodles of business.

Another reason I don't place a great deal of emphasis on open rates: Opens don't always get counted. Because tracking software requires people to view images, and a lot of email software doesn't show images by default, the actual number is usually higher.

One very effective (but often overlooked) metric you can track is the click-to-open rate for your website. Clicks represent a great way to test which recipients are the most active; in fact, you can actually see what they open and click. It's those clicks that best predict someone's interest in what you have to offer. After all, people who click are engaging with you and taking another step in building the relationship between you.

You also can use clicks-to-open to test email subject lines, by finding out which line brings you the highest open rate. Play around with this over a few months. What is most effective? However, please be careful: just because a subject line is popular doesn't mean that particular email will bring you any more business than one with a lower click-to-open rate. In the end, it's the content—and your offering—that translates to business growth.

To boost click ratio, I tell all my clients to put links in their emails. Here are a few easy, non-invasive ways to use links that your customers will love:

- Create an offer. Give them a reason to click through. That might be a special offer on a product or service, or it might be something as simple as a link to a free tool available on your website (a quotations engine or listings search, for example).

- When you set up your email newsletter, create evergreen, permanent content that stays there each month. Use these spots to put links to offers or to the most popular or important parts of your website.

- Add links within relevant articles. At the end of one or more articles in your newsletter, create links that go to a page on your website with further information on that topic (or details of a product or service you offer that relates to the topic.)

- Use buttons as well as links. These can make your links more obvious and appealing. The more links you have, the more opportunities you've provided for people to click, and the better chance you have of converting clicks to sales.

THE TAKEAWAY

Email newsletters can be very useful to test your marketing. But be careful how you perceive and use the numbers. Even though anti-spam legislation is complicated and a bit time-consuming, it protects legit marketers like us. At the end of the day, email newsletters, like any other form of relationship marketing, should be about building long-term relationships with clients. Keep adding value and doing all the other stuff mentioned in the previous nine chapters and you won't go wrong.

THE EXERCISE

Consider the ROI for emailed newsletters using the methods noted at the beginning of this chapter. Spend some time with your financial statements and your email list. Can you separate revenue for different marketing channels? If so, figure out your Revenue per Subscriber (RPS.)

If not, try figuring the average cost per action (AC/A) comparing the costs of promoting a seminar via other media channels with the cost of using your email distribution list, by tracking actions taken by responders (i.e. signups to a seminar).

AND:

As appealing as email newsletters may seem, don't make your final decision just yet. Print is not dead, after all. The next chapter may convince you of the absolute value of print newsletters and the even more valuable option of using both—in different, but complementary, ways.

Had a surprising experience with your email marketing? I'd love to hear about it; drop me a note through the site: **www.AlwaysConnectBook.com**.

Mark Twain Got It Right —Print's Not Dead

CHAPTER 11

Most people would tell you that email is the wave of the future—that print is dead. But to misquote Mark Twain: Reports of direct mail's death have been greatly exaggerated.

You should still send emails to your clients and prospects. Emailing is great, as long as you do it right. It promises big results and it's practically free to send out. But that doesn't mean it's the solution for everything. And while social media's the hot new thing, many experienced and successful business owners continue to use direct mail.

Indeed, in our business we've seen a huge increase in requests for help with paper mailings. Some clients are actually saying, 'Forget email, just make me a newsletter for printing.' In an era where there is too much email, where there are fewer and fewer books, a paper newsletter can be a special, fun discovery in your customer's physical mailbox.

No, print is definitely not dead.

I'm not alone in thinking this: Recent research indicates that almost three-quarters of consumers prefer mail over other advertising methods. And 40% will try out a new business they discovered by receiving its direct-mail piece. That means lots of opportunity for businesses to capture new customers, simply by reverting to the tried and true techniques of postal mail.

A printed newsletter is a physical object, which is that much harder to ignore. There's something about being able to hold the letter in your hand that makes the communication much more powerful. It won't get trapped in spam filters. People are used to receiving paper mail, so it doesn't feel like an intrusion. Plus, an enticing and well-written paper newsletter is more likely to stick around for multiple readers to enjoy. It's "bathroomable."

Putting a physical object into the hands of your clients is very powerful. It's the next best thing to a handshake. Paper newsletters have a physical presence in one's home. (You definitely can't say that about an email!) This means they are more likely to be kept and acted upon, now or in the future.

And, as I like to say: Is it bathroomable? That is, might your customers take your newsletter into the bathroom? The original Sears catalog was printed with a hole at the corner of each page so it could be hung in the outhouse/bathroom. People would read it and when... er...done, they'd tear off a page to use as lavatory paper.

As unsavory as this sounds, if you can make your newsletter bathroomable, you've created a successful relationship-building tool: the newsletter is worthwhile enough to keep in the house instead of quickly passing it from mailbox to trash. The content is interesting and the newsletter engaging enough to keep the reader interested in those...special moments.

LOOK BEYOND ROI

But what about the return on investment? The ROI for print is lower than for email. The proof is in this report, produced by the Direct Mail Association and quoted in Print in the Mix, a print advocacy organization based at the Rochester Institute of Technology that monitors and reports on third-party research. Every dollar spent on print, the report found, resulted in $7 in sales. That compares to $28.50 in sales for every $1 spent on email.

Yes, email is more cost-effective. However, as Print in the Mix notes, there are other factors at play that make print not only feasible but worthwhile. The Direct Mail Association report concludes: "for every 1,000 existing customers receiving a direct-mail piece, 34 will respond on average. For email, the average response—measured by taking the click-through rate and multiplying the conversion per click—is 0.12%."

While printing costs are higher and the resulting sales-per-dollar-spent are lower, more people actually respond to print than to email. That makes the print medium very effective. For example, if it costs $500 to send out print newsletters, but you get three new clients, and each worth $1,000, then you are up $2,500 in profits from where you were before. If an email newsletter (which costs you pennies to put out) with the lower electronic response rate gets you just one new client, you are up only $1,000.

As Print in the Mix suggests, the continued effectiveness of direct mail has a lot to do with the quality of data and the ability to target paper mail more effectively. In AdAge, Yory Wurmser, director of marketing and media insights at the DMA, comments: "The quality of the response for direct mail also indicates that direct mail is not disappearing."

Your customers will appreciate that you think so highly of them that you want to splurge on a print newsletter. Print implies that business is going well, and you intend to continue as a fixture in the community—not a fly-by-night business that's online one day and out of business the next. Newsletters are all about creating and cementing the bond between you and your neighbors/customers. Like the old-fashioned hardware-store owner—the guy we introduced at the beginning of this book who knows his customers' needs before they do—you can be more than just a business, you can be someone's friend, or at least a friendly acquaintance.

It's all about creating and cementing the bond between you and your neighbors/customers—sort of like the old-fashioned hardware-store owner, the guy we introduced at the beginning of this book who knows his customers' needs before they do. You can be more than just a pillar in the business community, you can be someone's friend, or at least a friendly acquaintance.

Over the years, I've gained a lot of experience about what works... and what doesn't. These lessons don't just stem from my own experiences, they also come from clients' experiences. Here, I'd like to give you some more of the ideas that our members at Ready to Go

Newsletters have developed for their print newsletters. Print is tailor-made for these uses and these ideas prove it.

Let's start with a former Newsletter of the Year member. Remember him? His clients missed his daughter's joke—a regular feature in most of his newsletters—when he failed to include it. This member is a print enthusiast. Just try to imagine any online method of distributing newsletters in this personal and (obviously very successful) way:

> I deliver the newsletters myself to 700 households monthly. I distribute another 100 or so by mail and hand them out at open houses and to for-sale-by-owners. It's important that I put a face with the name—and the newsletter. One FSBO [for sale by owner] client listed with me after witnessing me delivering them. It was a $465,000 listing.
>
> My broker appreciates what I am doing to promote my newsletter so much that she pays for the copies and I use staff in the office to assemble the newsletter. It is a family affair. My wife walks 1/2 of the route and my daughter helps too. Her joke is what many people eagerly wait for.

For this member, print rules. But other Ready To Go members also appreciate the special properties of print:

- Using the newsletter like a business card. As soon as they meet a potential new client, they'll hand over a copy of their current newsletter, and ask if they may put him or her on the mailing list. Action idea: Keep copies of your newsletter with you wherever you go, yes, even in your car trunk or within your briefcase.

- Personalizing with local, relevant information. Community news and information is something any business can add. That's why you can leave your newsletters at any local library or even farmers' markets, medical waiting rooms, and other community gathering spots—it contains useful information that stands on its own.

- Contests with prizes. You can create your own contest with prizes sponsored by local businesses.

- Giving away space to charities. One client offers free advertising in her print newsletters to local charities for their upcoming events. It's a way to make the newsletter relevant while creating a feeling of goodwill in the community with community groups thankful for the free publicity—it's a win-win.

FIRST LESSON: BE STRATEGIC

One thing to watch out for with a print newsletter is the temptation to send out thousands of print newsletters to people not in your database. While this can work as a long-term strategy, a large mailing such as this necessitates deep pockets. The danger is that you will run out of money before you're able to judge whether your strategy is working.

Newsletters are for people who think long term. That's why we give a big break on Ready to Go Newsletters' prices to those willing to commit for a year. It's no good sending out just a handful of newsletters for a couple of months and then giving up. You'll never know if they would have worked or not. Leads from newsletters sometimes take months, if not a year or two, to develop. Here are some ways to use direct-mail newsletters and make sure you're thinking long term.

SEND YOUR NEWSLETTER TO YOUR CLIENT LIST

Sending newsletters to existing and previous clients on your distribution list is the cheapest, easiest and most effective way to use direct mail. It's cheap because you are probably not mailing thousands of copies, and yet it's still effective because you are approaching people who have already bought your services. If you have anything extra to sell to your clients, then it makes sense to keep in touch.

For example, if you are a real estate agent who would like to earn a second listing from a client, or an insurance agent who wants to write a second policy (or continue to collect residuals on existing policies), then it's a no-brainer to mail to your client list. This is your pool of eager, interested folks—consider them to be an untapped well of leads that will continue to be profitable.

What to do: If you have more than 200 subscribers, mail to your clients every month, using bulk or first-class mail. If you have a smaller number of subscribers (say, around 100), mail them first class from your office in an envelope.

SEND NEWSLETTERS TO LEADS

If you're always collecting leads—and unless you've got more business than you can handle, you should be—it's usually worth sending a printed newsletter to each recent lead. However, I always advise to qualify those leads. You should have a strong idea of the characteristics and behaviors of your ideal clients and spend the most marketing dollars on those people. And be timely. People are "hottest" and most interested when they first contact you. Strike while that iron is hot.

What to do: Mail to your leads every month using direct mail, but use analytics to be very aware of lead quality and behavior—you may need to adjust your mailings accordingly.

Mailing Fact

The more newsletters you send, the more likely you qualify for bulk-rate postage. In the U.S., the cut-off is 200 pieces, and it's a big drop in price.

A word of warning: In return for the lower standard/bulk rate, expect slower delivery and less accountability.

SEND NEWSLETTERS TO POTENTIAL LEADS

Until recently, I have been skeptical about sending newsletters to cold prospects. Unless you have a very targeted database of mailing addresses, you can end up spending a lot of money on printing and mailing—without the results to justify that expense. However, new products from the post office have made the cost of mailing much more affordable.

In the U.S., the USPS offers Every Door Direct Mail as an easy way to send to a group of addresses for a very low price. You can find out more about this and similar products at: www.usps.com.

In Canada, look into Unaddressed Admail and other programs at: www.canadapost.ca.

What to do: If you know your potential clients live in certain geographical areas, consider using these methods of mailing newsletters. Customize your newsletter to include information relevant to these regions, to better serve clients who live there.

SEND CUSTOM AND UNUSUAL NEWSLETTERS

While it's true that printed newsletters can attract more attention (and thereby clients) than other methods, you can go further and really stand out. Remember this from Chapter 6?

Simon Payn's Golden Rule #1 of
Newsletter Publishing:

Make your newsletters for and about your customers. Respect their time and meet their needs.

At Ready to Go Newsletters we've been working with clients to produce truly custom newsletters, in format or in content, and sometimes both. For example, we helped a real estate agent produce a newsletter for a particular condo in her city, targeted for those residents' needs, which helps her attract listings from within that building.

We are helping another agent become an expert in his neighborhood by producing a newsletter filled with market stats and listings.

Newsletters don't have to be the standard 8½ x 11. You could also do a newsletter that looks like a newspaper, or one that's on a postcard. What better way to stand out than trying something different? With modern printing technology and design software, you can do almost anything you imagine. Remember though, sometimes less is more. Don't spend so much time working on design that you shortchange the content—quality, personal content gives your newsletter the biggest impact.

PLAIN VERSUS BEAUTIFUL

A simply designed newsletter—which could be just text on a page—can be much more effective than something very beautiful and fancy. After all, this is all about authentic communication—it's not about looking pretty. Sometimes plain is best!

The newsletters we make are quite plain in design. That is deliberate. Think of the letters you open in the mail. They are mostly just text. They say something important, so you read them. Compare that to highly designed flyers that look more like promotional material, and something you'd be likely to trash rather than read. Of course you don't want your newsletter to fall into this camp!

PROFESSIONAL LOOK

Use highly skilled writers, good proofreaders, and a designer who understands simple, effective design. Use boxes to make certain elements stand out, if you wish. Make sure everything is readable and that it fits together nicely on the page. Make it clear the newsletter is coming from you. Include your contact info.

If you send your newsletter in an envelope, regular laser paper is fine. If it's a self-mailer (without an envelope), have it printed on high-quality paper. This is the place to spend a bit more if there's room in your budget—if your newsletter looks scruffy after being savaged by the post office's machines, it reflects badly on your business. I recommend 80# paper, and consider printing with a coating to protect against smearing and tears. Leave room for the mailing address and indicia (the coding on paper mail that substitutes for stamps—you can get specs from the post office). Near the address, include a teaser for what's inside to encourage people to open it.

Simple is okay! With both professional and home printing, it's often much cheaper to print in black and white. One benefit of black and white is that it will look like something that's meant to be read, not a promotional piece.

THE PRINTING PROCESS

You certainly don't have to spend a lot of money with a printer. If you're printing fewer than 200 newsletters, you can easily handle that at home, at the office, or one of the big box stores. This can be very cost-effective, especially if you're printing in black and white and mailing the newsletters in envelopes. Format-wise, this also means you don't have to worry about leaving space for the mailing address or stamps.

Once your mailing list expands and you're printing more than 200, it's worth hiring a commercial printer. With a professional print service, the more you print, the cheaper it is per newsletter. Printers also provide services like collating, folding, stapling, and even cleaning up design issues.

WORKING WITH A PROFESSIONAL PRINTER

John A. Giles III is a consultant and technology director for CPrint® International, a professional alliance of North American independent printing companies that work jointly to achieve higher industry standards. He's been involved with the printing industry for more than 30 years. Who better to tell you how to work amicably with your printer?

"One of the most common mistakes you're likely to make is creating your publication before talking to the printer about budget," says

John, in an article written for Microsoft. He suggests discussing your newsletter program with your printer before you create it, "to keep costs down and avoid production delays."

Your budget should factor in the software you're using to generate the newsletter, and the way you plan to deliver the file—will you be walking in with a flash drive or emailing it to the printer? Do they have a file format that's easier to work with? Will you need to convert your file or will they do that for you? By following your printer's recommendations for formatting the file, you can save a lot of time, money and heartache. Your budget should also include the total numbers you're printing, whether you'll use offset or digital printing (more on this below), the paper choice, and the method of binding/stapling/folding your newsletters.

OFFSET VERSUS DIGITAL

These days the print quality is just as good whether you use offset or digital printing for your newsletter. The difference lies in the cost and run size. Offset is the process of printing on a press using ink. This has a one-time setup cost, no matter how many newsletters you want. The initial cost has a larger impact if you're printing fewer copies. Printing more newsletters, the setup cost is spread out over the greater number and the per-unit-cost drops, making offset a less expensive way to print larger runs. A digital printer uses toner and has almost no setup costs, allowing you to print as many or as few as you want. But digital is a more expensive way of printing larger runs, which may factor into your decision. John recommends that if you're printing more than 500 copies, opt for offset printing.

Get quotes from a couple of printers but don't automatically go for the lowest price. It's worth paying a little more for a print service that will be your true partner. Just as you want to be there for your clients, you want a printing company prepared to work with you, including helping you spend your money wisely.

Printers can offer a lot of value-added features. A good local printing company will take the time to check for typos or for headlines missing a word or two. A local company can also help you choose the right mailing list. They likely have experience with local mailings and can even assist in finding the best mailing price. The right printer will help you through the process with a minimum of fuss, and allow you to meet your timeline and budget requirements.

But—and this is important—be aware that printing takes time. You can't just send the file to a printer and expect to put newsletters in the mail the next day. A good printer will have other jobs, and they'll need to schedule your job, so make sure you have a realistic sense of the time involved. As part of your selection process, provide a draft timeline and ask how long in advance they'll need your files for each newsletter. Take these recommendations to heart and meet your deadlines. Missed deadlines can be inconvenient for you, lead to rush fees or delayed printing, and ultimately erode the relationship with your printer.

A savvy printer can suggest how to keep costs down while still putting out a good product. "The right printer for you is the printer who becomes your partner in the printing process," John says. "Better printers make you look good in print and do it on time and on budget."

VARIABLE-DATA PRINTING

In the past, hyper-personalization has been a pipe dream for small businesses. Now, thanks to variable-data printing (VDP, also known as VIP for Variable Information Printing), many print-solution companies are making it easy to customize on a realistic budget.

VDP is what prints your phone bills and credit-card statements—anything that requires a big chunk of custom data inside a frame of information that everyone gets. Until recently, VDP required expensive programming and just wasn't practical for less than thousands of copies. Now many companies have developed solutions that cost less and can be spectacularly successful.

With VDP, you send the printer a properly prepared file using a specific software package that supports VDP and handles your database. The company can then personalize your newsletter for with different content for different regions or even individual readers, without having to change or slow the printing process. It could be as simple as a mail-merge that greets each client by name, or you could include unique graphics for each interest group or demographic. Maybe there are photos and illustrations of families in the newsletter you send to parents of young children, for example. Or you have a Home Improvements section that goes to recent home-buyers, that's replaced with a Mortgage Qualification Made Easy section for potential new buyers.

Customer-specific information is almost like talking one-on-one to each individual reader. This isn't as expensive as you might think. While it does raise the cost, your ROI will likely spike, making it a bit more feasible for those of us without deep pockets as we launch our first newsletter. Personalization makes your newsletter more likely to be read, retained, and acted upon. Quoted in an article for MultiChannel Merchant, Nicky Milner, vice president of program management for printer Transcontinental, says returns for a fully variable print job range from two times to 15 times the rate of return for a static job.

You probably already have a wealth of information on your customers. Frankly, if you can manage it, I think VDP is terrific way to build a one-on-one relationship with customers.

PRINT'S ACE IN THE HOLE

The great thing about print newsletters is that, as I said at the beginning of this chapter, they are physical. In someone's briefcase or on their desk, your newsletter is a physical reminded of your business relationship. Carried with you, they become a calling card that's more engaging and effective than a simple business card. Newsletters can be left at a coffee shop, library, school or in the waiting area of your place of business. You can include a printed newsletter along with your product, as The Country Hen does ever so well (as described in Chapter 4). You can work with other local businesses to combine marketing and make complementary offers in your respective newsletters. What could be a simpler, more elegant and cost-effective solution to getting it out there than this?

Finally, this quote from the Direct Mail Association makes powerful good sense:

> It's important to remember that it's not a case of print vs. digital. Rather, each channel, employed properly, can give a powerful boost to all the other methods used in a campaign. Today's sophisticated marketers keep emotion out of the decision-making process and allow the numbers to indicate how best to invest their marketing dollars. And every marketer should be working to optimize their efforts across all channels—including print—to create the most powerful mix for ultimate success.

I couldn't have said it better myself.

THE TAKEAWAY

Printing your newsletters can connect with customers and prospects in a way that email can't. It's worth using both and taking advantage of each method's unique characteristics to cover a much wider audience. Variable-Data Printing allows you to put your carefully segmented distribution list to good use, by inexpensively hyper-personalizing and building on personal relationships with your customers (a theme I've been discussing throughout the book, that I bet you've caught on to!).

If you don't want to constantly manage this double distribution process or put in numerous hours to write and produce your newsletters, there are excellent alternatives to tailor-make your newsletter. Ready to Go Newsletters is one, but there are others out there too.

THE EXERCISE

Here's a bit more blue-skying for you. Imagine a perfect world in which you send wonderful, interesting, useful newsletters maintaining solid relationships with your regular customers/clients and attracting new ones. In this perfect world, you get $9 for every $1 spent (not a bad ROI!), and talk-show hosts want to find out just what you have done to be so successful.

Based on what you've learned here so far—and there are still important chapters to come, such as Chapter 12 on auto-responders—prepare for these TV or online appearances with a presentation. Write down the steps you took to make this work so well. What were the reasons you did what you did? Describe the factors that influenced these decisions. Don't worry about charts or graphs, just simple words will do. The point is to get this information into one place. You can tweak or polish it up later.

The catch: Make your presentation like a long elevator pitch. Ninety seconds tops! This will help you focus powerfully on the most important parts of your newsletter marketing—the elements you truly care about and should make sure to include in your newsletter plan

AND…

I'd very much like to see and blog about your "presentation," maybe even include it in a follow-up to this book. So send it to me via email, postal service, fax, courier, text… or direct my attention to your LinkedIn or Facebook accounts or your website, where (I hope) you've posted your presentation and called it: My Perfect World. You can get in touch at **www.AlwaysConnectBook.com**

Newsletters On Autopilot

CHAPTER 12

What if, once you put the time in behind the scenes to build it, all your email content went out automatically? That's essentially what autoresponders are all about.

With autoresponders, the idea is to put as much of your marketing as you can on autopilot. The minute someone signs up to receive your emails, a series of queued-up messages are triggered to sail into his or her in-box at specific dates and times. For example, the first message welcomes them to the list and provides a sign-up bonus. The second message arrives after one day; the third after four days; another after seven days, etc. Each message is sent out automatically unless the recipient unsubscribes (which hopefully does not happen!). Best of all, the system can send different messages and take actions depending on the response of the client or prospect.

You can use auto-responders in many ways. Here are just a few:

- To nurture leads
- To capture new customers
- As payment reminders
- As special scheduled content
- To support your loyalty program

Marketing expert Perry Marshall writes, "Autoresponders are one of the best—and by far, one of the most economical—tools to find and build relationships with potential customers. Slowly, methodically, and inescapably your messages build their trust and their interest until suddenly, bam, there they are...calling you...emailing you back... turning into paying customers."

Autoresponders are a great way to attract new clients. For example, you can offer giveaways and information on your product or service without having to write a new offer every time. By writing and designing this content once, you can send it out to as many subscribers as you like. It doesn't matter when they sign up, and you don't have to keep track of who's new and who already has the information—the autoresponder does that. You can distribute coupons to encourage trial runs of your products or services and easily track how successful each one has been. You can start to build a relationship.

AUTORESPONDERS FOR NEW LEADS

First, create a form on your website encouraging visitors to sign up to download something valuable and useful. For example:

- You're a real-estate professional. Someone goes to your website and sees an advertisement for a 10-day virtual course on things that home buyers in their neighborhood need to know.

- You're a life coach. Potential clients visit your website to download a planner for Five Days of Happiness, with journal-writing prompts and activities to achieve happiness.

- You're a financial planner. When you give your card (or your latest newsletter) to people you meet, you encourage them to visit your site and download a checklist that helps them assess their retirement plans.

Immediately after filling out the website form, your new lead will automatically receive the download link, or an email with the valuable offer they've just requested. Then, over a series of autoresponder messages, they are thanked for signing up, provided the several days' worth of lessons or information you've promised, and encouraged to contact you with comments or questions. Even though you aren't there in person, the automatic messages are written to convey how friendly, enthusiastic and engaging you are (or how responsible, energized and focused).

Meanwhile, the autoresponder system has tagged this person as interested in first-time buyer information, or improving their happiness, or planning their golden years. That person is added to a particular segment of your database.

Of course, each message should include a call to action. For example, "Are you interested in receiving information about real estate in your city? Click here for information about the market and the latest listings." With that click, the reader is added to another database segment. A few days after receiving the listings, this subscriber might receive another message suggesting he check out a graph of relevant housing prices in the neighborhood, over the past 10 years. Then maybe the autoresponder follows up a few days later with a message about the best ways to secure financing.

Each nugget of information sent out gets more and more specific. Each message builds upon the previous. With a one-time effort on your part, you're able to give tools, advice, and valuable, useful information to every new person who signs up to receive your updates. Meanwhile, you're going about your day, doing business with new and repeat customers. It's as if the autoresponder functions as your personal assistant—contacting new leads for you, until the potential clients are ready to take action.

This lets you keep your services, products and expertise in the front of their mind while your potential client decides where, when and what to buy. By the time they're ready to choose a product or service provider, you've already established yourself as a credible, helpful, and highly knowledgeable person. Whether you're a life coach, a broker, or a real estate professional, you'll be at the top of their list.

SETTING UP YOUR AUTORESPONDER

Whether you're nurturing or prospecting, the autoresponder set-up is pretty simple. You can write the emails once and then forget them, which makes good use of your time—and multiple uses of your content. Try re-using content from your published newsletters.

An insurance agent might have been sending out newsletters for several years, filled with articles about various types of insurance. This agent could repackage those articles and into sequences full of useful advice for people specifically interested in auto insurance, or annuities.

You already have the content, so make it work for you.

It's also easy to offer sets of unique messages for the different segments of your mailing list. For example, a real estate agent could have a series for first-time buyers, a series for young families, and a series for pet owners. When you deliver material tailored to your readers' interests, you're more likely to engage them as an expert—someone who cares about what they care about.

Timeliness is another feature of the autoresponder. When you first meet a new potential client, that's when they're most likely to spring for what you have to offer. In a busy day, it's hard to make time to follow up with new leads very often. With the autoresponder, you can keep in touch right away, and in a way that's not pushy—you're giving them valuable information that they've asked for.

In a program of regular newsletters, informative emails can fill in the gaps. The best autoresponder messages are usually on a single topic, and what's called "evergreen" content—not tied to a particular month or year. Use your monthly newsletters for the most current and newsy information, then keep the relationship going with educational resources—courses, whitepapers, special charts—through the autoresponder.

Finally, autoresponder messages are easy to "design." They're often sent in plain text rather than HTML, or at the very least, in a lightly designed format.

"CALL ME, MAYBE ..."

After you've built up a new relationship (or reinforced a longstanding one) through your autoresponder, how do you know when the about-to-be client is ready to buy? Simple—they'll tell you. Of course each message has a "contact me" link. When the client wants to get your services, they let you know they're ready! You'll immediately receive a note from the system to call and set up a meeting or take an order. You can also set up your program to notify you to call new mailing list members when they sign up—this doesn't have to be right away, it could be after seven days or after their first online purchase, just to ensure customer satisfaction.

Does all this make you concerned that you're contacting your leads too much? That's a valid concern, but it comes down to the value of the content. Think about how many emails everyone receives in a day (a lot!). Your emails are one of many, but that's not what causes leads to unsubscribe. People begin to experience "email fatigue" when they're no longer interested in what you're sending them—it's irrelevant, it's not new to them, maybe the content's boring them out of their skulls. The important thing to remember is that you must offer value. If you don't, readers will soon unsubscribe and you've lost those potential clients.

Yes, it is possible to overdo it. Too many messages will swamp your prospects—they'll start to resent the inbox space you're taking up. Don't get me wrong: for some businesses it's okay to send something daily, but it must be part of a well-thought-out strategy. The emails must be useful and important. You must let your subscribers know in advance—when they sign up!—that it's a daily subscription, so there are no surprises. And you need to monitor the responses closely.

Despite all the research available on autoresponders, there really isn't a definitive answer on when people develop message fatigue. Everyone's tolerance levels differ. However, there is one excellent way to sense potential fatigue and that is through your analytics. When 'opens' and 'clicks' from a particular subscriber start to decline, you may be looking at someone who is beginning to disengage. And it's especially important to notice when disengagement happens with people who historically have opened and clicked, but for some reason no longer do. This is where a professional email marketing firm can help you, by suggesting ways to freshen up your content, make it more useful, and position it as welcome to your readers.

ONE-SHOT MARKETING

On the other side of the stratosphere from message fatigue is one-shot marketing. That's when businesses send out one message, and that's it! This often happens when prospects give their address to receive some information, the software automatically shoots them an email with the information...and there are no more messages.

In my opinion, this is a big waste, and a bunch of missed opportunities. It's pretty hard to capture, intrigue and convert today's increasingly savvy buyers with a single message, especially if they don't know you well. It had better be a darn good message if you're relying on just one attempt to woo them—like, stone-tablets-on-the-mountain good. With autoresponders, I believe that slow and steady wins the race. I've actually had autoresponders going to some people for at least a year before they suddenly contact me and make a purchase. It's amazing and incredibly gratifying to feel that a long investment in my customers' well-being has paid off. People often take time to make buying decisions—don't rush them along! Instead, make sure you're constantly engaging them, and monitor those clicks and opens.

FOLLOW UP MADE EASY

One weakness many small businesses have is in their follow-up. Especially for 'solopreneurs,' there just isn't sufficient time to keep on top of marketing efforts. But with the right software, you don't really have to struggle to keep up. As in the earlier case of the real-estate agent who was educating clients, it can all be done automatically, and in a much more powerful and sophisticated way than on your own.

Many companies have yet to discover all the many options available with Marketing Automation Software (MAS). This is a new category that's about to take off, and it's the next generation after autoresponders.

With MAS, you can get very specific and granular in the type of information you send out, and the info you get back in analytics. The software takes care of database management so that there is much less manual followup for you to do. With only a few tweaks to your content and customization depending on the segment's interest and behavior you can automate almost all of your predetermined steps.

I use a service called Infusionsoft to do a lot of my marketing automation. People sign up for various types of information and are tagged appropriately to be sorted into interest- and demographic-based segments. If, for example, they've requested printed samples, they're filed according to the specific samples they've requested. Their names and contact information show up on a dashboard, and my MAS then sends out the response. By not having to supervise or click or write new content every time, I am removed from this process, leaving me time to handle other things in my business.

It doesn't stop there. The MAS is set up to trigger other responses once the information has been sent out, and not just followup emails! For example, the next step could be a reminder that shows up on my dashboard with the client's information, so I can call to confirm they received the information and ask whether they have any questions. Infusionsoft's MAS does the work that I could not feasibly do on my own or that would require so many staff that it would no longer be affordable.

MORE NEAT STUFF

With marketing automation software, I can identify my hottest prospects according to criteria I set. For example, I can score a particular person by how many of my autoresponder emails they open, how many links are clicked and what pages are visited. Talk about making it easy!

Perry Marshall (the marketing expert) often teaches about using automatic marketing. He has a concept called "the Maze"—an interlinked series of messages that a business owner can develop with autoresponders. He says this is "THE critical feature if you want to build multi-step marketing sequences for different products and promotions."

Here are his Maze points:

- The Maze is what gives me the ability to have very specific target communication with my audience.
- The Maze automatically adjusts the frequency of my emails to fit what my audience wants.
- The Maze focuses my messages to what each member of my audience wants to receive.

Basically, the Maze is different series of autoresponder messages and sequences. Subscribers select for themselves the information they wish to receive, based on their interests. If they're offered something, and they click on it, they get it. It's as simple as that.

Imagine building a whole maze of personalized content. Each prospect can take a different pathway based on their interests. Just think how much authority you can build with someone by sending all this useful information directly tailored to them. Of course, when mapping out your maze, carefully match the products you offer to the content you send. These should be comparable pairings. In other words, the person would definitely like to receive both product and content and doesn't consider one to be ancillary or non-relevant. You could start with a sequence about one product, then during that sequence ask if they are interested in another related product, then send information about that—don't try to jam them in all in one place.

SOFTWARE OPTIONS

Now, as amazing as marketing automation software is, not everyone needs the most high-tech package right off the bat. In fact, simple autoresponder software will do the job just fine, especially as you're first building your list. It needn't be complicated. Start with one sequence and build it out from there. Or, if you're adventurous, map out something complex in advance—but it can get confusing quickly.

Some email service providers offer auto-responders and/or MAS: Aweber, Infusionsort, Ontraport, Marketo and Active Campaign are all options to explore. The marketing-automation industry is on the rise. There will be more to come.

THE TAKEAWAY

There are two REALLY BIG takeaways from this one small chapter!

First, people signing up for your autoresponder have chosen to let you into their lives. They are telling you what they want to learn about your product or service. Essentially, you're nurturing your leads.

Second, if you give your readers what they need and want, they'll buy from you—perhaps again and again. You're converting leads to sales, and focusing your time on those who are actually ready to take action.

The autoresponder really is your very best friend. As MAS becomes increasingly sophisticated, you'll find yourself just short of coming face to face with new clients. Your regular clients will feel totally nurtured and cared for, too, with very little effort or expense on your part. It's a marketer's nirvana. But if you still want the personal touch (and just maybe a soapbox of your own), I recommend a combination of auto-responders or MAS and freshly written content.

Today's programs in customer-relations management are designed to work together—and when automatic responses are done right, they're very powerful indeed.

THE EXERCISE

Blue-skying time: What parts of your business could be automated to make your marketing more effective and/or save you time and money? Let your imagination go. Remember to consider the recipient of your imaginary sequences of messages. Put yourself in your prospect's place and go back to basics: Will your automated messages be interesting and useful? Are you pushing too hard and overwhelming your recipients? What's the sweet spot, both for your readers and for you as the writer?

AND:

If you'd like a look at my auto-responder emails, come sign up at **www.AlwaysConnectBook.com**

Making Your Newsletter Pay

CHAPTER 13

Let's get down to brass tacks. "Selling" isn't a bad seven-letter word. Selling is how you—and most people—earn a living. Thanks to selling, you're able to connect valuable products or services to your current customers—and to customers-to-be.

So when somebody (like me) says, with urgency: "You need to sell in your newsletter," please don't feel guilty. Your newsletter is indeed a way to reach customers, maintain relationships, provide useful content and approach new clients. But it's also a way to make money. Without money you can't do any of those things mentioned above. Without money, the hard work and effort—and, yes, cash—you put into your newsletter isn't worth a hill of beans.

Surprisingly, some people are afraid to practice sales skills in their own newsletter. This doesn't make sense on any level. If you think your client not only needs your product or service but will also benefit, it's a natural transition to move from educating them (as you have been doing in your newsletter) to offering them the opportunity to buy something that will continue to make their lives easier.

You need to make your newsletter pay—or it's simply not worth publishing.

HISTORY OF SELLING

Consider what I am about to say as a history lesson, but with a business-savvy twist. Way back when, we humans began bartering. Maybe one caveman exchanged his rock collection for an animal skin he couldn't stop drooling over, or he swapped clubs with a fellow caveman. And so it went until around 1100BC, in China, when metal objects (money) began to be exchanged for goods.

The concept of selling—that is, providing something you didn't make, for money rather than for another good or service you personally needed—only began in earnest with the introduction of manufactured products. During the Industrial Revolution, demand for factory-made goods rose, and spawned a whole new class of salesmen to sell these products. Unfortunately, before statutory law was implemented, consumers were regularly disappointed by shoddy goods sold by snake-oil salesmen making false and misleading product claims. This gave rise to the stereotypes of the sleazy traveling salesman, the fast-talking salesman and so on.

It wasn't until 1916, when the First World Congress of Salesmanship was held in Detroit, Michigan, that salespeople were actually encouraged to win their customers' trust, rather than just promoting the virtues—real or imagined—of their products. However, this idea didn't gain traction until the late 60s and early 70s, when salespeople began to realize that it was the customer who actually holds the power. That it wasn't enough to say how great the product was—you had to win over the customer. Salespeople discovered they could sell better if they aligned a product's benefits with customers' needs. Advertising and marketing strategies began promoting products as solutions to problems. The focus shifted to proving that your product solved customers' problems better than your competitors' products.

With better demographic research, salespeople targeted their product messages to the specific groups of consumers they thought were most inclined to buy the message and the product—strategic selling via enhanced technological methods.

Now, in the second decade of the 21st century, we're experiencing another revolution. This one is all about technology: analytics and marketing automation software make it super easy to identify, build relationships with, and focus solutions on the customer. And not just any customer, but the best customer, the loyal, lifetime buyer. As with the Industrial Revolution, this has revolutionized the process of selling.

Some people, like Forbes contributor Mike Myatt, suggest that traditional selling is dead—or, if still alive and kicking, should not be.

Says Myatt, "Call me crazy, but I don't want to talk to someone who wants to manage my account, develop my business, or engineer my sale. I want to communicate with someone who desires to fulfill my needs or solve my problems. Any organization that still has "sales" titles on their organizational charts and business cards is living in another time and place, while still attempting to do business in a world that's already passed them by."

Is this the case? What does the future hold for the companies Mike Myatt is talking about? What about the rest of us? By now, I think you know my bias: While I certainly don't see a eventual demise of traditional selling—there always will be a place for trading money (or its equivalent) for goods—I do see a much-needed change in the approach to selling.

You might call this "back to the future." I foresee a future where everything old (about selling) is new again. Where one-on-one relationships—enhanced with new generations of intelligent automation—will be the only way for small businesses (or any business, really) to survive. It's a return to the old-fashioned customer service we've talked so much about in this book.

How do you make your newsletter the brightest in your industry? It's all about the carefully thought-out offer.

MAKE THEM AN OFFER THEY CAN'T REFUSE

An offer (or promotion) is an essential tactic in your marketing tool kit. It's effectively an extension of your goal to educate prospects and customers.

Free offers can be very effective in generating leads. Take, for example, an offer of a free seminar to new-home buyers who sign up to receive a newsletter on a real-estate agent's website. The seminar—and the content of this agent's newsletter—should be designed to educate prospects on aspects of the industry and the services he offers. Using offers to generate leads should remain a key part of your marketing program.

However, at some point in the selling process you want the customer to move from a passive reader to an active buyer. An offer can be a call to action. If it's relevant, well-thought-out and timely, it will change your relationship with the customer, from "person who gives me great information" to "person whose services are going to make my life better." The transition can be natural, so that your customer/reader will consider your offer value-added content, and not sales pressure. Of course, even after converting the reader into a client, you'll still be educating—providing useful and important content that your prospects and customers need. From here forward your focus for them will be on serving and nurturing existing customers rather than mining for leads.

UNSELLING

"There are three hundred and sixty-four days when you might get un-birthday presents—"
"Certainly," said Alice. "And only one for birthday presents, you know."

- Lewis Carroll, Through The Looking Glass

Much like the Mad Hatter's unbirthday, you're transitioning from educating to unselling. It's as vastly different in intent and design from yesterday's sleazy salesmen as Alice is from the fantasy creatures she meets in Wonderland.

Here's how to segue from educating to selling—seamlessly:

- Ensure your newsletter content remains new, fresh and different. Just because you're including an offer in hopes of turning a reader into a buyer doesn't mean you can neglect the rest of your content. Especially at the delicate stage of conversion, your newsletter content needs to be useful and valuable. At Clickz.com, Jeanne Jennings notes an industry standard of 60%-or-more editorial compared to 40%-or-less promotion and sales.

- Be low-key. Make the transition very gradual and natural. If you're already providing interesting useful content, this shouldn't be difficult. Just don't suddenly start every article with a paean to your products or services.

- Use your autoresponder. Ensure you tailor offers to the needs of your customer, just as you've tailored your content to their interests and concerns.

- Here's the tricky part: Know when to stop educating and start selling. Where is that sweet spot in the selling process where the customer is teetering on the brink of buying?

- As you forge a relationship, you've been learning more and more about that reader. What will it take? What conditions must exist in order to make him or her decide to buy your product or service?

You're looking for the customer's hot-button issue so you can sell the perfect product or service to solve it. Like the hardware-store salesman in this book's introduction, you intuit your customer's needs, perhaps before he or she even realizes it. Only you are able to offer just the right solution at the right time and the right price.

At the risk of sounding repetitive, it's about good customer service. Over time you've nurtured this relationship. You've educated your customers, you've sent reminders, and you've made them smile and think. You've even made your newsletter bathroomable. Now it's time to get them to buy something from you. This is when you leverage your hard-won relationship with your customer by implementing a call to action.

Take, for example, a financial advisor (let's call her "Alexandra") who uses her newsletter to help educate clients and potential clients with interesting, investment-focused articles. These articles have likely raised questions, concerns and interest in investing. Many are now considering Alex the go-to expert on investment strategy. In a box at the end of a particularly interesting article on a new investment strategy, she might include the following:

"Hi, Jan: I thought you might be interested in learning more about the new investment strategy I've touched on in this article. Check out this white paper I've written focusing on this strategy. I'm making it available as a download to my newsletter readers only for the next seven days."

Like the customer-focused hardware store owner, or the real-estate agent who offered herbs from his garden as he walked around distributing his newsletters, Alex is providing old-fashioned customer service. She's become the trusted friend who answers questions and educates via her monthly newsletter. She's segmented her customers, so she knows exactly what each needs and wants. Even though it's a virtual relationship, they feel like they know her one-on-one.

Through relationships carefully built over several months, Alex (and you) can target offers like consultations or services to customers who are ready to buy. Remember, an offer needs to be specific and should include an expiration date. Alex's call to action has a great chance of success because it's built around trusting relationships—and because the offer is good.

OFFERS THAT WORK

Seven out of 10 consumers say they've used a coupon or discount they've received in a marketing email. Even so, it needs to be the right offer at the right time at the right price. What does a good offer look like? How do you create one that 70% of your audience will likely buy into?

Let's start with defining a market offering and work from there. A market offering is a combination of products, services, information or experiences to satisfy a need or want. This definition is simple and to the point, but may be a bit short on answering the whys and hows. In fact, your offer can be pretty much anything you provide to your existing customers already, but with the ultimate goal of encouraging a new lead to try it out. It may include discounts, free tools, consultations, or buy one/get one promotions.

Your offers need to support your objective. If you're seeking new customers, educational material such as ebooks, seminars and webinars, and industry research will encourage new sign-ups. On the other hand, if you've already built a relationship and want to include a call to action to move the process a step further, a coupon or free trial is more appropriate. Just make sure it's a solid offer.

You can make your offers through virtually any vehicle that works for you, but since we're discussing newsletters, those are great places to introduce an offer. You can also make offers in media advertising, in-store promotions, on your website and via social media. You can even get carried away with outdoor billboards or even skywriting if you have the funds and really want to impress. Or you can use all of the above.

These days, it's not just about having one offer. The process is much more sophisticated, Don't be a one-hit wonder who captures customers but doesn't retain their business. If you want to take full advantage of selling in your newsletter, it's about building a plan with multiple offers clearly targeted, and tracking them so you can instantly see what offer goes to whom, and when. This isn't something you can build overnight. Know that the behind-the-scenes work is taxing, and may take a month or two to build, but the results are worth it. Your time and energy investment will pay off as customers act upon the offers they're receiving while you go about an average day running your business.

Be consistent. All your marketing materials—especially your offers—must reflect the business you're in and complement it. While a free seminar or a consultation shouldn't be all about your brilliant service or awesome products, it certainly should imply that your product or service will solve problems. (Note that these could be problems they may not even have known they had!)

Make each offer valuable. If you're using the offer to generate leads, it has to be compelling because people are often wary of providing their contact details. Make it stand out and lay out all the reasons why you are asking for contacts, taking time to stress how you can make lives better.

If you're still at the nurturing stage with your newsletter readers, you may not want to change your winning formula. A valuable offer carefully presented could be perceived by your readers in much the same way as a valuable article. Go low-key if that's been your mantra so far and it's worked well for you.

For each offer you should include a call to action—one that will work for all of your readers, or all your readers in that particular segment—as did the financial advisor in the example above. For example, if you're an electrician and your newsletter includes an article entitled "Are You at Risk from Improperly Installed Electrical Outlets?" accompany the article with information about your guide to electrical safety and offer a discounted home-safety check-up. Don't just knock a buck off the regular purchase price. It should be a genuine—and good—discount that matches a genuine—and good—product.

If you have a particularly strong offer targeted at multiple recipients, send it in your newsletter but also take it a step further by supporting it on your website and in social media. Track the impact of each offer with your analytics software. Only through tracking will you be able to learn which of your offers worked best, with which groups and how well. Then you can design similar offers with a reasonable expectation of success.

Some examples:

- Offer a product of the month or a special service (such as a first-time home buyers' seminar offered by a real-estate agent).

- Provide a discount code or printable coupon. Make it worthwhile—these days many retailers offer up to 40% off a first purchase (online or in-store) when a prospect signs on to receive a newsletter or lists special interests in a form on the retailer's website.

- If you are a small retailer, offer a larger discount in a "now-or-never" promotion for products you may be phasing out.

- Don't forget to provide a start date and an end date for the coupon or discount code. Use your emails to remind customers a few days ahead of the end date for the discount. You never know, you may get enhanced traffic (and sales) as a result of that last-minute push.

- Offer free webinars or seminars, and use your newsletter to invite readers. You can either send the invitation to your entire distribution list, or pick two or three categories from your segmented list, choosing people who are particularly interested in the topic (like first-time home buyers). Leave the issues of your printed newsletter containing the invitation in hubs around town to encourage new readers to sign up. This is a great way to build your distribution lists.

- Provide links or other ways of easily accessing product catalogues or lists of your services. You don't want to present this amazing opportunity and then not have the information about your overall business immediately available. That would be like a tease, right? Include all the ways to contact you.

- Try summarizing the event in your next newsletter, giving some key benefits that were received, and announce future dates.

PLACING YOUR OFFER

Where exactly do your offers go in your newsletter in order to create maximum bang for your buck, without annoying or misleading your customers? For example, say you include a "How to" article in your newsletter designed to keep your customer reading…and learning. It makes sense to put an offer at the end of this article. Particularly with this type of content, it's a logical jump from reading about a new investment strategy, for example, to discovering an offer for your white paper on this very strategy. Think of it as continuing their education and not just you suggesting an offer. Remember, too, that many people will read a how-to and think, "That's great but I don't want the hassle of doing it myself," so the end of that article is also a great place for an offer that involves them hiring you to carry out the techniques!

Like the financial advisor, you can make this offer at the end of the article without coming across as annoying or pushy. Think about it: if the person is interested enough to read the article, then it's a logical conclusion that he or she wouldn't mind hearing a sales spiel. In fact, because it's such a smooth transition, your offer will likely be met with enthusiasm and action.

An upfront approach may work, too, but only if you do it in context. As writer Sean D'Souza points out in his Psychotactics blog, you can place your offer right at the beginning, before the reader even gets to the article. "That too—amazing as it may sound—is natural. We like to know what we're in for. Treat it merely as an announcement—akin to having an agenda, or a table of contents, and it won't be perceived as a real intrusion," Sean notes . The place NOT to put your offer? The middle of your article where it interrupts the reader! Have you ever been annoyed when a commercial comes on in the middle of a show you're enjoying? With an article, a sales pitch halfway may discourage the reader from finishing, and cause frustration, even anger. Obviously that's NOT the response you want for your offer, especially when you're trying to encourage your loyal readers to take that next logical step…to buy from you.

CROSS PROMOTIONS

Once a reader has become a customer, you can (gently) cross promote, by both both upselling and cross-selling. These two terms are often used interchangeably, but they aren't exactly the same. Both types of offers can be made at the point of sale, in a follow-up email, or on the online order-confirmation form. In both cross-selling and upselling you're turning a single sales opportunity into a more lucrative one. And if it's done with the customer's interests in mind, you're actually increasing the value of the purchase.

Online or in person at the point of sale, you can suggest the purchase of upgrades or complementary items based on what the customer has just bought. Consider the offers made by many large online retailers during the purchasing process, such as: "Others who have purchased Product X also bought..." or "You also might like Product Y." That same approach can be used to encourage the customer to trade up to a better product before signing on the dotted line.

In cross-selling the customer is offered the opportunity to purchase a related product, perhaps one that isn't specifically connected to your core business but still relevant. Let me walk you through an example: a life-insurance agent may suggest a client also purchase auto insurance or homeowners' insurance through him or her. The agent, who from the previous sale now knows and understands the client's circumstances, will be able to suggest the right insurance product at the right time. The advantage to the customer? They've already consulted an expert for their first purchase; now there's no need to sort through hundreds of options to find the right fit for their next purchase. The agent is saving the client time and, hopefully, money.

You can often work with a partner on cross-selling offers, by suggesting the purchase of appropriate products sold by a partner—maybe something like access to a special online manual to accompany the purchase of a new electronic device. Both of you can promote the offer in your newsletters and online. Then you both benefit when customers buy your product and your partner's.

Upselling is encouraging the customer to purchase a higher-level version of the product he or she was already intent on on buying—such as a more expensive watch or an upgraded smartphone with all the bells and whistles. Bear in mind, the customer must perceive it as an offer of value that's an important part of their decision right now. Otherwise you may come across as not listening and just trying to make a bigger sale. The upgrade must be something the customer really wants or needs, an option for a better product that's important to consider before making the final purchase choice.

Take, for example, an interior decorator who offers her client a special piece of furniture that will enhance the original design. It costs extra—but if it truly completes the look and elevates the design, the client will spring for it. The attention to detail may also make this client more inclined to use the same designer for future projects, which is the start of a beautiful relationship.

From here, it's a short step to leveraging your upsell and cross-sell options into offers. If it's an important offer to you and your customers, it definitely deserves some promotional support.

ADVERTISING

You also can seek partners who will pay to advertise in your newsletter, because of your high-quality distribution list. Maybe they want to tap into a different demographc and you hold the keys to reaching those people. Selling advertising through your print or email newsletter may or may not work for you, but if it's a good fit, it can provide a steady stream of income, new customers for your advertising partners and an additional source of useful information for your customers.

If you're publishing a local newsletter, choose a non-competitive partner who complements your business and is located in the same area of town. You're looking for a company with an very similar business philosophy to yours, but a different (and complementary) product. Definitely don't recommend someone to your valuable customers if you're worried that the business won't fulfill its promises—I can't think of a faster way to put your relationships with customers at risk. Your advertising partners must also be providing information that's valuable and relevant to your clients.

Tips to make advertising work for you:

- Look at what your own offers have achieved. Are your readers more interested in coupons and discounts than product trials or e-books? Your experience can help your advertising partners determine the best offer.

- Don't sacrifice editorial (or your own offers) for a partner's ad. Placing a partner's ad too prominently could disrupt your own content. Ensure it's visible and doesn't interrupt the flow of your design.

- Use a design element to differentiate your partner's offer from the rest of the content. Perhaps a box with the word "advertisement" in small type, or a subheadline, "From our partners..."

- Stay with the objective of providing additional value to your customers, while keeping this your vehicle for communicating with them. Consider a small "editorial" announcing your intent to provide additional useful and valuable content and introducing your ad partner.

- Work with your partner to track the ad's effectiveness. While this constitutes valuable analytics for your partner, it also gauges your customers' response. If, for some reason, you get unsubscribes or complaints, you will want to reconsider partnering together again.

PAID SUBSCRIPTIONS

Again, this approach may not work for you, but many have made it work successfully, a few of my clients included. Ben Settle, who we discussed in the previous chapter, combines free daily emails with a paid newsletter subscription for more and even better content.

In a world of free newsletters, why would someone pay to subscribe to one? Take a look back at Chapter 1, What is Your Why. Remember Simon Sinek's quote: "The goal is not to do business with people who need what you have—the goal is to do business with people who believe what you believe."

People will pay for a newsletter because they believe what you believe. It's as simple as this. They want to identify with your philosophy—not just your approach to doing business—but your world view too. Notes Sinek: "We follow those who lead, not for them but for ourselves."

If people are willing to pay to subscribe to your newsletters, it's quite possibly not because of your products, or even your interesting and useful content. It could be that they yearn to feel a part of something bigger than themselves. Like Volkswagen Beetle fans or Apple enthusiasts, this is a strong, compelling feeling that can airlift a brand into success.

Products have a vital role to play—they make belonging to this club "cool." Software producer SendBlaster wrote in its blog: "Readers of popular blogs like Cult of Mac or AppleInsider are also expressing a similar degree of kinship, but this time with a commercial brand. The information they find on those pages lets them feel that they know more than most about something that many people find cool and desirable." As form follows function, your newsletter content can align with this "cool" image. This will do more than attract more subscribers. It increases the take-up of the offers you make. It's hard to make your newsletter into this kind of pay-for product, but you don't have to be Apple to make people feel special. After all, that's what we've been talking about throughout this book.

For example, one real estate agent I know attracted paid subscribers by presenting his personal, colorful answer to one industry-related problem in every newsletter. The rest of the newsletter contained useful, interesting content that his readers appreciated, but what made it worth paying for was his outrageous commentary. Readers were interested, amused, annoyed—but sufficiently engaged—to want to pay money to find out what problem he'd deal with next and, more importantly, how he'd deal with it. He became a very successful storyteller, so much so that the thrill was in his delivery and the message flew under the radar as something to be absorbed, but not "the main attraction."

THE TAKEAWAY

It's important to make your newsletter pay! Selling is how you benefit from your close relationships with your customers. Sell appropriately, with regard to those relationships and with a conviction that what you have to offer is a great deal, right now. And track your offers to know their impact and offer your customers the things they want and need most.

THE EXERCISE

Think of 10 upselling, cross-selling or partner offers you can make over the next 10 months. Can you do something special for the holiday season? What about back-to-school or summer-vacation promotions? During downtimes, would these give you and your sales a boost? During peak sales season would they capitalize on momentum? Can you use offers to get rid of costly inventory that hasn't been selling?

Consider the objectives: the what, where (placement in your marketing materials), when, to whom, and how to promote each offer. Write it all down in a spreadsheet or on a piece of paper. Make it easy for you to act upon later.

Then just do it!

AND:

While all of the chapters in this book are intended to help people who want to make good, useful newsletters, this chapter may be the most important. As I said at the beginning of this chapter, without selling in your newsletter, all your hard work—and all the information in the last 12 chapters—will be wasted. This is Lucky 13, because it helps you make money. You'll also make your customers and prospects happy at the same time. Win-win!

Have you got a great offer idea? Tell me about it at **www.AlwaysConnectBook.com**

The Ultimate Marketing Machine

CHAPTER 14

As I've said repeatedly throughout this book, your newsletter can't be created—and experience overnight success—in splendid isolation. Your marketing must also support your newsletter, and your newsletter must be a key part of your marketing plan.

Here's a puzzle for you: If you could view your marketing approach from way up there at 30,000 feet, how would you describe it? Would you say it's scattered all over the place—a newsletter here, a website there? Or would it look like a well-oiled machine with all your marketing programs working in harmony and your perfect customer at the center to receive it all?

One of the saddest things I've seen is a really fine business, with a great product or service, that crumbles thanks to a scattered marketing plan. Yes, the business owner has a website. And yes, he or she has a Facebook page (but doesn't update it regularly, or understand how to make sure posts get seen) and yes, that owner sends out a monthly newsletter.

But when, after a couple of months, the owner hasn't gathered leads or locked in any sales, we can safely determine it's due to failed marketing. But is it the newsletter's fault or the website's? Is it just the wrong time? The wrong demographic? I've even had a business owner ask in frustration, "What's wrong with my customers anyway?"

It's not your customers. It's the dramatic change in today's marketplace that has altered your universe. But there's hope. You can use these changes as your tools instead of fighting against them. You can find your own genuine voice and way of interacting with customers, using modern marketing to succeed in your business journey.

Let me just sum up a couple of key points you've learned—but from a personal, modern marketing angle:

- Today's customers look for authenticity. Remember the importance of transparency and trust in building a long-term relationship with customers?
- Today's customers seek out authorities—go-to experts who can help them find and buy the perfect product to meet their needs.
- Today's customers want to be—if I can use an old-fashioned word—courted. They want to be nurtured, and have limited patience for businesses who can't or won't nurture relationships.
- Today's customers expect a thousand points of contact—sure, that sounds bit extreme, but many people now expect to do business with someone who will communicate with them through Facebook and Twitter, in Google ads, in person and through email, in print and on YouTube, in blogs and articles.

Understand today's customer and you'll find the building blocks for success are right in front of you. What remains is to snap those blocks together in a tight, personal, interactive marketing campaign to maximize your chances for success. To win in today's market, you need to understand—and play into—today's customers. Easier said than done? Not really. With the tools you've gained in the previous chapters, you're ready—ready to build your Marketing Machine.

THE QUINTESSENTIAL MARKETING MACHINE

If you think back to the story of the owner of the old-fashioned hardware store, you'll see that his story still speaks to today's customers: the one-on-one relationship, anticipating customers' needs, being the go-to expert. These nostalgic approaches are alive and well in the 21st century. What's changed is the way customers want to be nurtured—through those thousand points of contact. Today you need a marriage of the old-fashioned hardware store owner's approach—your overarching focus is your customer—with the modern technology that make it all happen seamlessly and easily. That combination is your Marketing Machine.

It seems obvious (now that you're deep into this book) but your Unique Selling Proposition (USP) must remain the underlying theme of your Marketing Machine. Only by differentiating yourself, carving out your niche and being brave enough to ask the "Eulogy Question" (What would my customers miss if I went out of business?), will you be able to develop a Marketing Machine that uniquely reflects you.

Let's look more closely at the Marketing Machine and you'll see how it all fits together. With your newsletter at the center of it, this machine is designed to collect and nurture leads until they become clients. Once they buy into your products or services, the machine continues to nurture them by encouraging them to buy from you again and again. Keep in mind that the oil in the machine is the one-on-one relationships you're developing with customers.

LEAD GENERATION

The beginning of the Marketing Machine is your funnel. This is the place where you collect leads—your sign-up page on your website, plis all the places you collect contact information that goes into your database. Without leads you can't make sales—but from the research institute Marketing Sherpa (www.marketingsherpa.com) comes this startling statistic: 68% of B2B organizations have not identified their funnel. Where are the best/most leads coming from? They just don't know.

Where are your leads coming from? What's your funnel? Is it the business breakfasts you're going to once a month, the contact list from your community organization, or are you already using some good online sources? The leads you collect must come from a variety of sources, including those generated by advertising online, and off–line sources such as direct-mail postcards. For example, advertise on search engines such as Bing and Google. With strong keywords, the vast majority of the clicks pouring in will be from people hungry for what you've got. Or advertise on Facebook, where you can find people who share interests with your best clients. They may be at the same life stage as your best clients. Heck, they may even live where your best clients do. To find worthwhile leads, tailor your funnel to fit your individual situation. Once you've got a sense of where the best leads are coming from (using your analytics), only advertise in places where your most likely prospects hang out, to people likely to be interested in your products or services. You'll reduce your advertising and marketing costs because you'll only be talking to people who have a chance of becoming clients.

The next step is crucial: It's not good enough to bring in all these leads and simply route them to your website or a phone number. Most people will visit your website and never come back—unless you make the effort to capture contact information. That's where a good "lead magnet" comes in.

LEAD CAPTURE

A lead magnet offers something up front that is extremely attractive to your ideal leads. Something so attractive that they will be glad to send you their contact information in order to receive what you're giving them, Your lead magnet is so compelling that they will want to hear from you regularly through your newsletter.

If you've ever bought anything from Amazon you'll know how spookily perceptive Amazon's site can be. Browse something without buying and you'll probably get an email about it in a few days. Ads for this product will pop up in your Internet browsing too. Buy a book and you'll soon see a promo for another book just like it—maybe it's written by the same author or covers the same topic. Amazon does an excellent job of matching products to its customers' desires—one reason it has become an icon of marketing excellence.

The good news is: You don't have to be Amazon to create that kind of a Marketing Machine.

We've already seen some good examples of targeting in this book: a real estate agent might offer an in-depth guide to the market in a specific area—the very same area he targets with online and offline marketing. Or, if an agent targets seniors in her marketing, she might offer a guide for those over 55 who are downsizing. This kind of thoughtful targeting is what most of our successful clients do.

According to a recent study by Carnegie Mellon University, only 9.7% of study participants were comfortable sharing their email addresses with companies. Whereas, if you, like my successful clients, do it right, you can expect up to 30% to give you their contact information. That's pretty good compared to the 9.7% you'd get without a compelling magnet. That other 90.3% needs a damn good reason to part with their personal information. Give them that reason—through your vivid and personal story of how you are going to make their lives better. The higher the percentage of people who trust you enough to share their precious contact info, the cheaper these leads become because you're getting a much bigger bang for your buck. This means you can spend more on generating leads!

LEAD AND CLIENT NURTURING

Here's an interesting statistic from Marketing Sherpa: 79% of marketing leads never convert into sales. And another one: According to Verl Workman, president of Corcoran Consulting Inc., almost half of leads never get followed up. While Vern's article about this for RISMedia addresses real estate agents, this is applicable to almost every business niche. No wonder so many great companies fail to live up to their potential!

Why is this and what can we do about it? The researchers at Marketing Sherpa found that lack of lead nurturing is the most common cause of failure to convert leads into sales. What's sadder, as a survey from the market research firm Capterra points out, is that more than a quarter of marketing professionals—the guys who get paid for their expertise—don't even know their own conversion rate.

Is there something wrong with this picture? I certainly think so. Here's how it should go down. Once your leads are in your database—and qualified and segmented—you simply send the information your visitors seek. Then you keep in touch on a regular basis with your newsletter, auto-responder sequences, and relevant (attractive) offers.

In other words, you nurture those individuals, and keep nurturing them, for weeks, months, even years, until they are ready to buy. Because you've been courting them, you'll always be their first choice. There are many companies that can provide the services to do parts of this process, and there are others (including my company, Ready to Go Newsletters) that can put together your entire Marketing Machine.

What's most important, however, is to remember the basics: that you are in the middle, as the caring, knowledgeable expert. You're helping your leads and clients by providing useful and entertaining information on a consistent basis– just like the guy in the old-fashioned hardware store. There are many tools to help you achieve this. But at the end of the day they are only tools. Nothing can beat the magic that comes directly from you—that certain something that makes you unique and ensures you are the number-one choice among your ideal clients.

When you start to look at business this way, not as a cat and mouse game where you snare unwitting customers but instead sharing something that makes a big improvement on people's lives, everything becomes easier. And when it gets easier, it gets more fun. Honestly? It's a reason to jump out of bed every morning.

THE TAKEAWAY

Encourage people to join your newsletter distribution list/funnel by offering something compelling enough to meet their needs.

Tightly target your desired clients (bless the software that perfectly segments your distribution list!). Don't worry about numbers. You're better off targeting a small demographic perfectly than trying to be all things to all people.

Make your marketing genuine. Make it about your business, your clients, and the real and personal connection created between them.

Need Help Writing A Newsletter?

CHAPTER 15

Throughout this book I've described how to be your own publisher. The previous chapters have been all about crafting your newsletter: The Who, What, Where, When and Why of it (with lots of Hows and How Muches, too.)

I hope I've given you the recipe to produce a successful, interesting, useful newsletter at a reasonable cost that will make you money. I want your your clients and prospects happy and know that you do too.

But if this isn't your thing, if you don't have the staff or resources, and especially if you don't have the time, fear not: there's still a way to do it.

With ready-made, fully customizable and editable newsletters, my company is proud to help business owners produce their own print and email communications. We believe in making newsletters that are 'successful, interesting and useful at a reasonable cost that will make you money … and your clients and prospects happy.'

Just like you'd make if you had the time, right?

OUR BATHROOMABLE NEWSLETTERS

Sometimes people ask me why our newsletters are sort of disingenuous—and they don't mean that in a good way. Our competitors' newsletters are slick with fancy pictures, multiple typefaces and—worst of all—content lifted from somewhere else. You know those kinds of articles. The newsletter senders run the risk of their readers saying, "Wait—I already saw this," and putting it down. And who wants to work with a copycat?

I'm pretty sure that, if you've read this far, you aren't crying out: What's wrong with that? I guess I'd say, everyone to his (or her) own. We each run our operations differently, and over the past 13 chapters, I've pretty much explained why. Still, here's the way I approach newsletter publishing:

First, we only use specialists to write about the subject matter we cover. These are often second-career writers who have worked in their industries for years and now write, with enthusiasm, about issues facing their industry.

Second, our copy is guaranteed to be original. We have a dedicated copy editor who comes up with many of our story ideas based on her extensive journalism and public-relations background, as well as a love of reading and a genuine commitment to clients. Before any copy leaves her hands it has to meet her high standards. And then she runs it through a website designed to catch content that has been copied and not attributed. This ensures it is original. Then the copy goes to a proofreader and a production team.

Third, we give all our clients the opportunity to alter content in any way they wish. Want to add a sentence or two to the article? Done. Replace one article with another from our extensive archives? Done. Despite all this flexibility, I'm happy to say adjustments don't happen ofetn: we're very careful that our content is relevant and important.

Effectively, our newsletters can be anything our clients want them to be. The common thread is that they are each a strong part of a Marketing Machine. As I said at the beginning, your newsletter—however excellent—can't stand alone. At Ready to Go we don't just make wonderful (I believe) newsletters. We also know how to make them part of your unique Marketing Machine.

We can design a complete unique Marketing Machine for you, or create individually tailored packages: A Lead Generation package, where we'll help you use your marketing dollars wisely to capture good quality leads; a Lead Capture Package, where we'll encourage your prospects to give up their contact information, and a Lead and Client Nurturing package, where we'll help you use those 'thousand points of contact' to stay in regular touch with your prospects until they buy—and beyond. We'll look after all of it—or just the parts you need

For more information on our newsletter services, and to sign up for some free bonuses (see what I did there?), visit **www.AlwaysConnectBook.com**.

And if you liked this book—or if you think it could use some improvement—please leave us a review on Amazon. Your reviews will help me reach more people like you!

ABOUT SIMON PAYN

I started out as a journalist, working for daily and national newspapers in the United Kingdom and Canada (The *Birmingham Post*, The *Sunday Telegraph* and The *Toronto Star*). I edited news stories, laid out entire pages, and prepared articles to post on the Web. I rewrote stories, developed catchy headlines, and made every sentence as accurate and readable as possible.

With the advent of the Internet, I went to help start up an online publishing company in Amsterdam. Expatica serves people in several European countries by supplying information and community. As editorial director, I created six websites that were updated daily. It was an exciting ride—we built something from scratch that continues to help thousands of people every day.

Being part of that start-up gave me the entrepreneurial bug. To prepare for going it alone, I studied sales and marketing—with an emphasis on direct marketing—because without understanding how to get clients, you can't have a thriving business.

Now, the happy marriage of my journalism background and marketing skills is Ready to Go Newsletters. I found a gap in the market for professionally written newsletters featuring a strong marketing component. I couldn't be happier.

If you'd like to keep in touch, please visit this book's website at **www.AlwaysConnectBook.com**. I'd love to hear about your passion, your plan, and how you're making newsletters work for you.

ACKNOWLEDGEMENTS

A book is a bigger project than the 200-odd pages you have here would suggest. So there are many people I'd like to thank.

First, the wonderful editor at Ready to Go Newsletters, Frances O'Flynn. Not only does Frances commission and edit the articles our clients receive every month, but she also put many hours—no days, weeks—into this book, turning my writings, thoughts and musings into the product you see here. This is her work as much as mine.

Thank you also to editor Allison Williams, who battled corrupted files and corrupted sentences to turn out a polished final product, with the help of designer Jay Ashworth.

I also want to thank the marketing experts who have had such a big influence on my business and my thinking, among them: Dan Kennedy, Perry Marshall, Glenn Livingston, Terry Dean, Ken McCarthy, Jay Abraham, Paul Lemberg and the late Tom Hoobyar.

I owe a special debt of gratitude to my amazing team at Ready to Go Newsletters—Mayna, Kyla, Taiseer and Heather—who keep the ship running when I am too busy or too cranky to help. When I talk about customer service, I'm talking about this team. They rock.

Finally, thank you to my clients at Ready to Go Newsletters who are working the "system"—sending out newsletters month in, month out and reporting their results. These are the people I get up for in the morning; they are my Why.

Made in the USA
Middletown, DE
18 January 2020

83402606R00113